Quilt A
TRAVEL
SOUVENIR

Kimberly Einmo

American Quilter's Society
P. O. Box 3290 • Paducah, KY 42002-3290
www.AmericanQuilter.com

Located in Paducah, Kentucky, the American Quilter's Society (AQS) is dedicated to promoting the accomplishments of today's quilters. Through its publications and events, AQS strives to honor today's quiltmakers and their work and to inspire future creativity and innovation in quiltmaking.

EDITOR: BARBARA SMITH

GRAPHIC DESIGN: ELAINE WILSON

COVER DESIGN: MICHAEL BUCKINGHAM

PHOTOGRAPHY: CHARLES R. LYNCH, QUILT PHOTOS AND PAGES 9, 12, 57, 78

        KIMBERLY S. EINMO, PAGES 3, 7, 19, 20, 21, 25, 26, 27, 33, 41, 44, 46, 49, 50, 52, 54, 57, 58, 79, 83, 85, 88, 100

        CHRYSTAL ABHALTER, PAGES 19, 90, 91, 92, 94, 96, 97, 98, 99

        KEITH ENGLISH, PAGES 101, 102, 104

        KELLY IRENE HICKS, PAGES 67, 72, 73, 74, 75A, 77A,

        KAY B. SMITH, PAGES 19, 34, 35, 36, 39, 43, 63

        JAY STATEN, PAGES 19, 75B, 76, 77B

Library of Congress Cataloging-in-Publication Data

Einmo, Kimberly S.

    Quilt a travel souvenir / Kimberly S. Einmo

        p. cm.

        Summary: "Suggestions, techniques and patterns for creating quilted souvenirs representing travel memories. Includes lesson plans section for teachers"--Provided by publisher.

        ISBN 1-57432-892-1

        1. Quilting--Patterns. 2. Patchwork--Patterns. 3. Quilts--Design. I. Title.

        TT835.E45 2005

        746.46'041--dc22

                    2005026087

Additional copies of this book may be ordered from the American Quilter's Society, PO Box 3290, Paducah, KY 42002-3290; 800-626-5420 (orders only please); or online at www.AmericanQuilter.com. For all other inquiries, call 270-898-7903.

Dedication

This book is dedicated to my husband, Kent,
and my two sons with all my love.

The Einmo family at Burg Nanstein, Landstuhl, Germany

ENGLISH ESTATE, sewn by Mary Flynn, RAF Lakenheath, England, and machine quilted by Carolyn Archer, Lebanon, Ohio. This is a variation of the ENGLISH ESTATE quilt pattern on page 68.

Contents

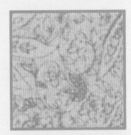

Introduction

I learned to love traveling at a young age. My parents, Wilbur and Nina Wallace, took me on many grand and unusual vacations when I was a child. I remember the sights and sounds from every trip, although my mother would probably tell you I saw only the backs of my eyelids from the rear seat of the car most of the time. We rode mules to the bottom of the Grand Canyon and learned to scuba dive in the Florida Keys. We rode camels to the Great Pyramids in Cairo, visited every battlefield east of the Mississippi River, and rode donkeys to the red-rose city of Petra, in Jordan. Come to think of it, we spent many of our trips riding on the backs of a wide variety of load-bearing animals during those summer adventures. After I was grown, I was fortunate to marry a man who was brought up to appreciate traveling in much the same way.

My husband and I have loved to travel since we were married in 1988, and we use every available opportunity to take a road trip, flight, or train ride to any destination. When I began quilting in 1991, we combined our vacation odysseys and weekend treks with the search for fabrics and quilt shops en route. And because Kent is a career U.S. Air Force officer, we've had ample opportunity to visit many urban, rural, exotic (and not-so-exotic) locations. Our sons expect lengthy visits at fabric stores and can make a game of picking up stray pins and threads off the floor, much to the delight of shop owners. They can even spot the perfect periwinkle print, if that's the current color for which I'm searching. (Gee, I hope they both grow up to marry quilters – because they are already "quilt trained." Their wives will be lucky young ladies!)

In August 2000, we had the ultimate good fortune to be assigned a military tour in Ramstein, Germany. This was a dream come true for us, and we took every available opportunity to travel and experience many fabulous sights, sounds, tastes, and textures throughout Europe. I became an expert at shopping on the Internet for fabric basics and the necessary quilting supplies I couldn't find locally. But I was a woman on a mission when it came time to discovering unique quilt shops and outdoor textile markets throughout the European community. It certainly seems like I've visited some of the remotest and out-of-the-way places on Earth while trying to follow directions written in languages other than English!

The idea for this book began during one of our frequent fabric shop stops, this time in Paris. My husband was pondering ways I could actually use my wonderful, one-of-a-kind (and quite often, expensive) fabric purchases from the countries we had visited, rather than let them languish uncut and unappreciated somewhere in my vast fabric stash. This set my mind into overdrive as I planned ways to showcase my fabric souvenirs, lace, ribbons, and trims in a special quilt from each country.

When we returned home to Germany, I began designing the quilts you'll find here, featuring some of those special textile treasures we bought during our travels in Europe. For countries in which I wasn't able to purchase unique fabrics, I incorporated blocks appropriately named for the region or nationality. It became a happy mission for me to design an entire collection of quilts by using aptly named blocks, a special theme, or an idea to capture the unique culture or feel of each particular country. I planned the quilts to look deceptively difficult, yet each is wonderfully easy to construct by using simple blocks, unique fabric placements, and clever block settings.

Thank you for joining me on this quilting travel odyssey. I hope you will enjoy these quilts, photos, and stories. No matter where you go, be sure to savor your own creative quilting adventure along the way. With every mile, step, or stitch you take, even if you never actually set foot beyond your own front door, remember to appreciate and truly savor every moment of your own unique journey.

My wonderful husband, Kent, pretending to be penniless following one of our international shopping excursions

shopping

Making Souvenir Quilts

Personalizing Your Quilt

When it comes to personalization and embellishments, I believe that pleasing yourself is the most important thing. These days, many quilters own mid-range and high-end sewing machines, and yet they seldom use the many beautiful, decorative stitches available at their fingertips. Do you own or have access to a computerized embroidery machine? If so, go for it — embroider your quilts to your heart's content. When making your own souvenir quilt, anything goes!

Here are some ideas to get you started. You can create a scene or an icon of a monument in a city you visited. You can use thread to stitch names and dates on your quilts. For a truly personal touch, if you have the software, why not scan a travel photo or postcard and digitize a memory to be embroidered on your quilt. If you aren't that familiar with digitizing software, or simply feel intimidated by it, start small. Use a simple line drawing and digitize a redwork-style (outline) embroidery design of the Eiffel Tower or some other recognizable landmark. Just jump in with both feet.

If you don't own a fancy machine, that's no problem. Use hand embellishments, cross stitch, or appliqués. Add buttons, beads, ribbons, doilies, or lace. Your quilt is yours to be sewn and personalized. It's *your* memory scrapbook. What a terrific way to capture your memories in fabric and thread to be savored and enjoyed for years to come.

In talking with friends and students from the classes I have taught, many of them have told me they enjoy collecting special fabrics from places they visit. But sometimes, special fabrics native to a particular region or area may not be readily available or even affordable. In this case, a wide variety of novelty print fabrics can be found in quilt shops, or from Internet shopping sources, that can be used to symbolize specific places or types of vacations.

For instance, bright tropical prints can be used to create a fun Hawaiian or island quilt; prints with bears, fish, moose, and other forest creatures will do nicely to represent a camping trip; and faux animal skin and jungle prints can depict a safari or even a local trip to the zoo.

Using special fabrics and novelty prints isn't the only way to create one-of-a-kind vacation memories. Why not choose blocks with names to represent places you've visited or things you've seen? This can be easy to do with the help of quilting software to aid in researching the quilt block names, or you can even search the Internet or your local library to find ideas for block designs.

Permission to be creative. With each quilt I make, I challenge myself to learn a different technique, to try something new, or to stretch my comfort level in some way. So, to offer you a boost of encouragement and perhaps help you learn a new skill or try a different technique, I've included a special section at the end of each chapter entitled *"TRY THIS ..."*. Don't worry if you make a mistake or if your experiment doesn't work out the first time. The important thing is to try. Think and work outside the box!

Gathering Supplies

FABRIC

The quilts in this book were made with 100 percent cotton fabric. However, when you are collecting fabrics from around the country or around the world, you'll find that there are many different fibers available. Consider incorporating other fabrics in your projects, such as silk, wool, velvet, and countless others because they may be the most representative of the particular region or country you are visiting. Try to learn as much as you can about them, such as the care and laundering instructions, from the local source. If fabrics are not available from a particular region, look for laces, ribbons, trims, and tapestries to incorporate into your souvenir quilts.

Hint

FABRIC QUALITY

The best rule of thumb is this: purchase the highest quality fabric you can afford. You'll be creating a lasting keepsake for generations to come, so you want to use materials that will stand the test of time.

SEWING MACHINE

Any sewing machine can be used to make the quilt projects, but keep in mind that your machine needs to be clean and in good working order. Before you begin, take time to carefully clean it with a lint brush. Don't blow into the bobbin-casing area to clean out the lint. The mechanical parts in your machine won't respond well to the moisture in your breath. Using a can of compressed air, try to angle the long, pointed nozzle so that the lint is blown out (from back to front) of the machine, not farther into the deeper recesses of the bobbin-casing area.

Following the instruction manual, oil your machine, if necessary. If you have not had your machine serviced in recent memory, then it is time to take it to an authorized dealer for a "spa treatment." You can use the time your sewing machine is being serviced to wash and iron your fabrics in preparation for sewing your project. Your machine will come back to you renewed and refreshed, and you'll be amazed how much quieter it hums as you sew. Make yourself happy with a fully functioning sewing machine. Nothing spoils the fun of quilting faster than a machine that keeps breaking

down, has tension troubles, or continually gets clogged with thread. Last but not least, begin each project with a sharp, new needle.

THREAD

I prefer using cotton thread with cotton fabric. For machine piecing, I choose a neutral color that blends with the fabrics, such as ecru, natural, or light gray. When working with a black background, I use black or charcoal gray thread.

Your sewing machine may work best with one brand of thread rather than another. Ask your dealer for recommendations or try several different brands until you find the one that works best for you and your machine. There are many new, exciting threads available today, so don't be afraid to try something new for your machine quilting and embellishments. Just be sure to test the threads on a fabric sample before sewing directly on your quilt.

PIECING FOOT

Several sewing machine companies sell a special piecing foot designed specifically for sewing ¼" seams, or you can purchase a generic ¼" foot. To buy a foot, you need to know what type of shank your machine has. Check your manual to see if the shank is low, high, or slanted. Contact the manufacturer if you have questions. Piecing with this ¼" foot will make all the difference in the world with your seams and will help ensure that your blocks finish at the correct size.

WALKING FOOT

For straight-line machine quilting, you will need an attachment called a walking foot, also known as a plaid matcher or even-feed foot. Some machines have a built-in dual-feed foot. The walking foot allows two or more layers of fabric to be fed underneath the presser foot evenly so that there are no pleats or puckers when you quilt.

FREE-MOTION FOOT

For free-motion quilting, you will need to use a free-motion or darning foot. The feed dogs must be lowered. Some machines come with an attachment to cover the feed dogs instead. With the feed dogs disengaged, you will have complete control over the speed and direction in which you move the quilt as the needle moves up and down. You may need to adjust the screw on your bobbin casing to achieve just the right tension for free-motion quilting. Don't be intimidated by experimenting with the tension settings.

Don't be discouraged if your first attempts are less than satisfactory. Practice a simple, random pattern of gentle curves and loops on a quilt sandwich made of leftover fabrics from your quilt top. You will improve the more you practice this technique.

Hint

LEARNING FREE-MOTION

For your projects, while you are learning free-motion, use a backing fabric in a busy print, which will hide your stitches much better than a solid color or muslin fabric.

BATTING

While there are many wonderful battings available, I usually use a thin polyester batt, one that drapes beautifully, or a thin 100 percent cotton or cotton-polyester blend. Read and follow the manufacturer's directions for pre-shrinking, if desired.

ROTARY CUTTER

Do yourself a favor and treat yourself to a new blade before you begin a project. You'll be delighted with a blade that can cut through multiple layers of fabric like a hot knife through butter. You can save used blades for projects like cutting wrapping paper (it makes wrapping gifts at Christmas fast and easy) or for your children's art projects.

Hint

STORING USED BLADES

A metal throat lozenge box (or one of those tins that holds those curiously strong mints) lined with a little leftover batting makes an ideal place to store your used blades until you need them.

ROTARY MAT

Always use a self-healing mat when cutting with a rotary cutter. The larger the mat, the easier it is to measure and cut large pieces of fabric. Try using your kitchen counter or other flat surface that is higher than a standard table. The extra height will be kinder to your back and allow you to cut, without pain, for extended periods of time.

ACRYLIC RULERS

Personally, I'm a ruler fanatic, and I like to use a variety of different rulers when I'm rotary cutting. At the minimum, you'll need a 6½" x 24" ruler, a bias-square ruler, and a 15" square ruler.

FUSIBLE WEB

Paper-backed fusible web makes appliqué quick and easy. It is best to choose a light- or medium-weight fusible web if you are using 100 percent cotton fabric. Be sure to read the manufacturer's instructions and test the fusible on a scrap of fabric before using it for your project.

SCISSORS

You'll want to have a variety of types and sizes of scissors on hand, including a good, sharp pair of shears and small, curved embroidery scissors. Be sure to have both fabric and paper scissors. Don't dull your favorite sewing shears by using them to cut paper.

One of the best presents you can give yourself is the gift of sharp scissors. I take my scissors to be sharpened every year during the week of my birthday. It's easy to remember to do this if you make it a yearly ritual.

MARKING TOOLS

A good mechanical pencil is a necessity, and chalk wheels in a variety of colors are quite helpful for marking templates, appliqué shapes, and quilting lines. Tailor's chalk also works quite well. I like those blue pens with disappearing ink. However, be sure to test them to make sure they really disappear from your fabric before using them directly on your quilting projects.

LIGHTING

Make sure your sewing and workspaces are well lit. The full-spectrum lights available today will make wonderful additions to your sewing area and are a welcome relief for tired, strained eyes. Invest in good lighting and save your sight.

IRON AND IRONING BOARD

A high-quality iron with steam capabilities is essential. Check the sole plate. If it is dirty or it has sticky, adhesive residue on it from previous projects, take the time to clean it with a cleaner made just for sole plates. If your ironing board cover also has the remnants of that sticky, fusible adhesive, wash the cover or invest in a new one. Your ironing board should be sturdy and placed close to your sewing machine, at a comfortable height.

STRAIGHT PINS

Straight pins are a must-have. The thinner pins will leave much smaller holes in your fabric. If your pins are bent or rusted, throw them out and purchase a new box. I like the flat-head flower pins because they are nice to use when I'm pinning seams and matching points. You can even iron over them.

A magnetic pincushion is a wonderful, inexpensive luxury. If you drop pins on the floor, just hold your magnetic pincushion upside down and wave it about 4"–6" above the floor. It will grab any stray pins and save your tootsies from getting stuck if you walk around the room in your stocking feet.

SEAM RIPPER

I've seen some of my students working much too hard and sometimes damaging their fabrics simply because they were using dull seam rippers or rippers with the sharp pointed tip broken off. Why struggle? Buy yourself a new, sharp seam ripper and always close the cap when you are finished, and don't be too hard on yourself if you do have to "unsew" a seam. Remember, no matter how careful you are, "as you sew, so shall you rip."

TEMPLATE PLASTIC

Essential for making templates, this thin, flexible plastic is available at most quilt shops and hobby supply stores.

BASTING SUPPLIES

Personally, I prefer to use a basting gun and a plastic grid (for underneath the quilt sandwich) for basting my quilts. Adhesive basting sprays are also efficient, and large basting safety pins are yet another way to effectively hold your quilt layers together. Try them all and choose your favorite method.

EMBROIDERY THREAD

There are many brands and types of thread, which will offer you a wide variety of results from your machine embroidery. One hundred percent rayon is typically the thread of choice for most computerized embroidery designs, because the sheen of rayon thread is stunning. However, there are also some excellent polyester machine embroidery threads that offer quite impressive results. Test your designs and thread choices first before embroidering directly onto your quilt blocks.

Hint

MACHINE EMBROIDERY, HAND LOOK

For outline embroidery or redwork-style designs, try a 12-weight cotton thread. It will look as if you did the outline embroidery by hand.

BOBBIN THREAD

For machine embroidery, I like to use pre-wound cotton bobbins. The thread is very strong, and there is almost three times as much thread in one pre-wound bobbin as there is on a bobbin you wind yourself. This will certainly help save you the aggravation of running out of bobbin thread in the middle of stitching an embroidery design.

If your machine has the option, turn off your automatic bobbin thread cutter while you are stitching embroidery designs. You do not want your machine to automatically cut the bobbin thread every time it stops for a color change. The bobbin thread should be continuous from start to finish on the underneath side of an embroidery design.

EMBROIDERY NEEDLES

Be sure to change your machine's needle frequently, since it wears out much faster when embroidering than when doing regular sewing. Use a needle specifically made for the thread and type of design you are stitching. For example, metallic needles should be used when embroidering with metallic threads.

When embroidering with metallic or other brittle threads that tend to break easily, embroider at half-speed, if your machine has that option. Slowing the speed decreases the heat and friction that can build up, causing breakage as the needle passes up and down through the fabric layers.

STABILIZERS

This may be the most unglamorous aspect of machine embroidery, but it may well be the most crucial. For professional embroidery results, you need to properly stabilize your fabric. Take the time to study and really learn about all the different stabilizers available on the market today. The basic rule is this: use a cut-away (permanent stabilizer) if your fabric has any stretch or give to it whatsoever, and use a tear-away (temporary stabilizer) if your fabric does not stretch in any direction.

I like to use an iron-on stabilizer on the back of 100 percent quilting-weight cottons. A water-soluble stabilizer is wonderful in the hoop when you are stitching lace designs. It rinses away completely leaving only the intricate design in thread. Experiment and become accustomed to using different types of stabilizers for different applications.

Favorite Techniques

WASHING FABRIC

As a general rule, every piece of new fabric I bring home goes directly to the laundry room where it is washed, dried, and pressed before it ever goes into my fabric stash. The washing and drying process removes excess dye, pre-shrinks the fabric, and helps set the color.

However, you may find, as I did, that there are times when it isn't feasible to wash some fabrics. For instance, the Dutch reproduction prints used in ICE TRAIN TO AMSTERDAM have a beautiful sheen, and washing them would remove the shine. Also, it would be terribly time consuming to wash the 100 or more 4" squares for a wallhanging, which probably would not need to be washed in the future anyway.

It is always better to be safe than sorry, so if you choose not to wash your fabrics, be sure to test for colorfastness by soaking a piece of your fabric in a glass bowl with warm water and the soap you plan to use for washing your quilt. If you find a fabric that bleeds, don't use it.

MY BEST TIP EVER

I love the feel of crisp cotton fabric when I sew. Because pre-washing removes the sizing, I like to use spray sizing when I iron my freshly washed fabrics. Nothing takes out wrinkles as nicely and makes your fabrics behave as well as spray sizing. Unlike spray starch, spray sizing is a synthetic, so it won't be a food source to attract insects, such as moths and silverfish. Spray sizing also makes your cut pieces cling together ever so slightly, and it helps to keep bias edges from stretching out of shape. You'll love the polished look spray sizing gives your patches and blocks, too.

STRAIGHTENING FABRIC GRAIN

I come from the tradition of tearing 100 percent cotton across the width of the fabric (selvage to selvage) to straighten the grain. After making the initial tear, I fold the fabric in half and make a straight cut approximately ½" away from the torn edge with my rotary cutter. I don't tear the fabric into strips for sewing, which would be much less accurate than using a rotary cutter and ruler, but by

ICE TRAIN TO AMSTERDAM, detail, quilt on page 20

making this initial tear before beginning to cut my fabric, I feel assured that I am cutting on the true, straight of grain.

PRESSING

Personally, I love to use a steam iron set on the hottest cotton setting when I press my patches and seams. Be especially careful when you are pressing bias edges, because steam can distort your patches and make them less accurate. Remember to press, not iron, your patches. By simply lifting up and pressing straight down repeatedly, you'll maintain the shape of your patches and keep your seams straight. Save the back-and-forth ironing for your clothes.

In the projects, all pieced seams are to be pressed to one side, not open. Start by pressing the seam allowances closed (or flat) before opening the unit and pressing the seam allowances to one side. This step will make your stitches contract and grab the fibers in your fabric, so the seam will be more stable and less prone to stretching or being pulled out of shape.

The little arrows in the assembly diagrams will show you the best direction for pressing seam allowances. If no pressing directions are given, press the seam allowances toward the darker fabric or in the direction that will create the least amount of bulk at the seam intersections. There will be instances in which you will have to make adjustments and press in a different direction to make the seams lie flat. Use your best judgment.

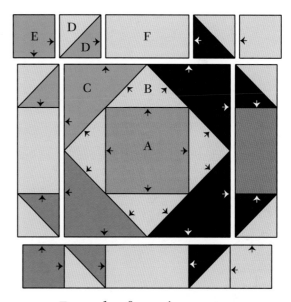

Example of pressing arrows

SHORTCUTS MAKE LIFE EASIER

I love notions and tools designed to make piecing and quilting more efficient and fast. New tools are introduced each year that provide simple shortcuts for making basic units. For instance, there are many different ways to accurately cut and piece half-square triangle units, including a variety of different rulers and triangle papers that are currently available. I would like to encourage you to try several of these quick shortcuts and new tools whenever possible. Pick your favorite ones and apply them to your projects.

If you are familiar with strip piecing, by all means, convert the pattern instructions to take advantage of this technique. With each quilt you make, I'd like to challenge you to learn a different method and stretch your comfort zone just a bit. You might find a better way to do something and have loads of fun in the process.

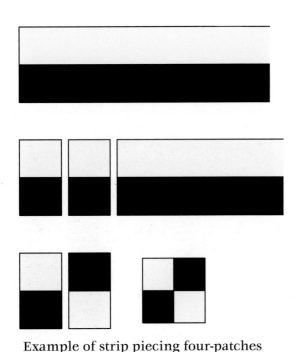

Example of strip piecing four-patches

NEAT MAKES PERFECT

I admit it, I'm a neat-nick, and I'd like to encourage you to become one, too. I believe in taking the time to trim all the little pointy "dog ears" and long threads from each of my patches and units before continuing to the next step in the process. As a result of having less bulk in the seams, your patches will lie flat and your points will match more perfectly, making all the effort worth it.

CORNER-SQUARE TECHNIQUE

With this technique, you can easily add triangle corners to rectangles and squares, without having to handle those tiny triangles. As a disadvantage, the corner-square technique uses a little more fabric.

1. Draw a diagonal line, corner to corner, on the wrong side of a square. Align the square in the corner of a larger rectangle or square, right sides together.

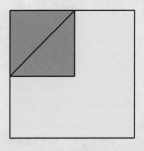

2. Sew along the drawn line. Cut off the extra fabric in the corner, leaving a ¼" seam allowance.

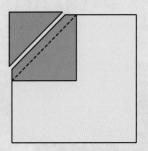

3. Press the triangle open.

IMPORTANT – squares sized for the corner-square technique are not large enough to use for making half-square triangles. If you prefer to use half-square triangles instead of the corner-square technique, add another ⅜" to the size of the square. For example, a 2" (short side) finished triangle, cut a square 2½" for the corner-square technique, but 2⅞" for making half-square triangles.

FUSED APPLIQUÉ

For all of the projects, the appliqué pieces can be fused as follows:

1. With a pencil, trace the appliqué shapes on the paper side of the fusible web.

2. Cut the appliqué pieces with paper-cutting scissors, leaving approximately ⅜" beyond the drawn line.

3. Follow the manufacturer's instructions to adhere the fusible web to the wrong side of your fabric.

4. Carefully cut the appliqué shapes directly on the pencil lines.

5. Remove the paper backing and position the shapes on the background fabric.

6. Use a hot, dry iron to press down on the appliqué pieces for a few seconds to fuse the shapes permanently to the background fabric.

7. You can leave the edges unfinished, but only if you plan never to wash your quilt. Or, you can finish the edges with a narrow zigzag, buttonhole, or other appliqué-finishing machine stitch.

MEMORIES OF GERMANY, detail, quilt on page 50

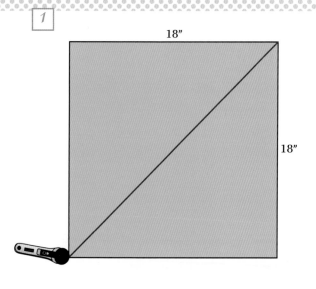

18"

18"

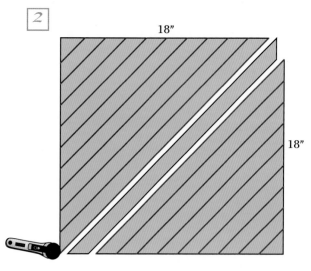

18"

18"

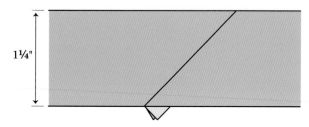

1¼"

1/4"
3/8"

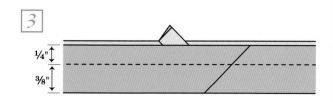

3/8"
1/4"

BIAS TUBES

Here is a simple method for creating continuous bias tubes for stems and other decorative touches. You will need a ⅜" bias bar for this technique.

1. To make a continuous ⅜" wide bias tube, cut the size square given in the project. Cut the square in half diagonally.

2. Then cut 1¼" strips, parallel to the diagonal cut, from both halves. Sew the strips together, end to end, to make a continuous bias strip.

3. Fold the strip in half along its length, wrong sides together, and sew the long edges with a ¼" seam allowance.

4. Insert a ⅜" bias bar in the tube and shift the seam to the middle of the bar. Press the seam allowance to one side so that the seam is hidden on the back of the bias tube.

FINISHING TIPS

After your quilt top is completely assembled, take time to clean up the underside by clipping excess threads or tiny "dog ears" that may be sticking out from seam intersections. Stray dark threads may show through light fabric and look unsightly once the layers are quilted. Press any seams that are not lying flat or that are lying in the wrong direction.

Consider how you will quilt the top and mark the quilting design on the fabric with a pencil, chalk wheel, or other marking tool. Cut the backing according to the pattern instructions and piece panels together if necessary. Press the backing and quilt top to remove any folds or wrinkles.

Quilt Patterns

QUILT SIZE: 49½" x 49½"

FINISHED BLOCK SIZE: 9" x 9"

ICE *Train to Amsterdam*

ICE TRAIN TO AMSTERDAM, sewn and machine quilted by the author

For our first trip to the Netherlands, we boarded an ICE (Inter City Express) train in Cologne, Germany. It was my first trip on a high-speed, luxury "bullet" train, and it was thrilling! We glided smoothly along at speeds in excess of 150 miles per hour through the picturesque country-side, where I saw my first glimpse of those famous Dutch windmills. We arrived a few short hours later in the charming city of Amsterdam. In a wonderful quilt shop there, Den Haag and Wagenmakers, which is located close to the queen's palace, I found some beautiful Dutch repro-duction prints. Immediately, I knew I had to make a Delft-blue quilt to commemorate this remarkable trip.

While this quilt looks elegant in traditional Delft blue and white, it will be equally stunning if you use the fresh, vibrant colors of the spring tulips for which Holland is so famous. Also, this is a great pattern for practicing your hand and machine quilting skills and to showcase some of the wonderful decorative stitches on your sewing machine.

Fabric Requirements

Yardage is based on fabrics at least 42" wide. Cut all strips selvage to selvage. Border measurements are extra long to aid in mitering the corners.

FABRIC	YARDS	PATCHES
White (background)	1⅛	12 A, 84 B, 68 C, 4 D, 8 F
Medium light blue	¼	16 B, 4 C
Medium blue	½	8 A, 40 B
Dark blue	⅝	28 B, 64 C, 4 E
Inner border	⅜	4 strips 2" x 41"
Middle border	½	4 strips 2¾" x 45½" (pieced)
Outer border	¾	4 strips 3½" x 51½" (pieced)
Backing	3⅛	2 panels 27" x 53½"
Binding	½	6 strips 2¼"
Batting		53½" x 53½"

ROTARY CUTTING

MEASUREMENTS INCLUDE SEAM ALLOWANCE

PATCH	MEASUREMENT
A	3½" x 3½"
B	3⅞" x 3⅞" (cut in half diagonally)
C	2" x 2" (see Strip Piecing Four-Patches, page 16)
D	2" x 3½"
E	1" x 5½"
F	3½" x 3½" (cut in half diagonally)

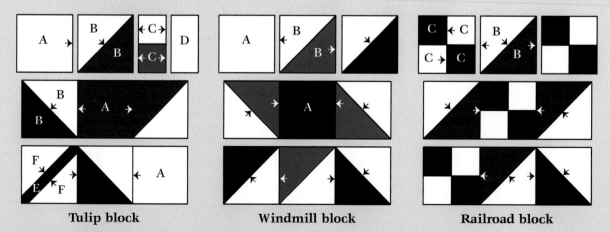

Tulip block   **Windmill block**   **Railroad block**

FIG. 1. Block assembly

Quilt Assembly

1. As they are needed, cut the patches listed in the Fabric Requirements table. (See the Rotary Cutting table for patch measurements.)

2. Referring to the block assembly diagrams, make four Tulip blocks, four Windmill blocks, and eight Railroad blocks (fig. 1).

3. Arrange the blocks as shown in the quilt assembly diagram, being careful to rotate the blocks to achieve the desired interlocking design (fig. 2). Sew the blocks together in horizontal rows. Then sew the rows together.

4. For each side of the quilt, sew the inner, middle, and outer border strips together. Treat the combined strips as a single border unit. Sew the border units to the quilt and miter the corners, being careful to match the border strip seams at the miters.

5. Add batting and backing then baste the layers together. Quilt as desired.

ICE TRAIN TO AMSTERDAM was quilted in a variety of methods, including some hand quilting, machine quilting in the ditch, and echo and free-motion quilting. Decorative machine stitching, through all three layers, was done on the inner border.

6. Use your favorite method to bind the raw edges of the quilt with the 2¼" binding strips.

FIG. 2. Quilt assembly

Hints
TRIM E/F UNITS

After sewing the flower stem (patch E) between the two F triangles, trim the ends of the stem even with the edges of the unit.

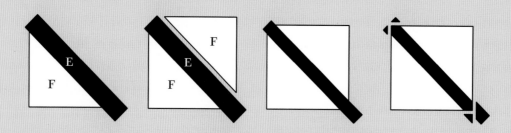

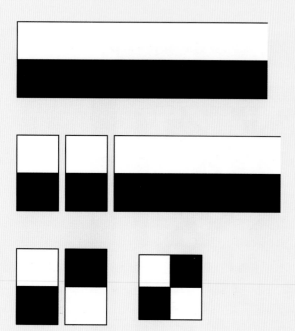

STRIP PIECING FOUR-PATCHES

For the Railroad blocks, the four-patch (4-C) units can be strip pieced as follows:

1. Cut four 2" strips across the width of the white and the dark blue fabrics.

2. Sew a white strip to a dark blue strip to make a strip-set. Make four strip-sets like this.

3. Cut each strip-set into 2" segments and sew two segments together to make each 4-C unit.

CHECK UNIT SIZE

After sewing and pressing your units, check to see that they measure 3½" before joining them into blocks. Remake any that are significantly smaller or larger than 3½".

TRY THIS ...

Many quilters are quite comfortable piecing their quilts, but they feel intimidated when it comes to actually finishing them. Do you currently have several pieced tops sitting on a shelf just waiting to be quilted? ICE TRAIN TO AMSTERDAM provides the perfect place for practicing a variety of quilting techniques. If you need to improve your hand quilting stitches, try quilting small areas in the windmill blocks or add definition to the pieced tulips.

The three outer borders provide easily accessible areas for practicing free-motion machine quilting, following geometric designs traced on the fabric with chalk, or sewing through paper that is pinned on top of the border itself. With this quilt, why not challenge yourself to try one new quilting technique, or at least improve your hand or machine quilting skills. You'll feel an immense sense of accomplishment when your quilt is completed.

Keukenhof Tulips

KEUKENHOF TULIPS, sewn by Claire Neal, RAF Lakenheath, England,
and machine quilted by Carolyn Archer, Lebanon, Ohio

Keukenhof Gardens

I've been fortunate to visit many wonderful gardens during my travels, including the world-famous Keukenhof Gardens located in The Netherlands. My first visit to Keukenhof was in late April, just as millions of tulips and other spring blossoms were at their peak. The 70-acre grounds were impeccably manicured, and with the sunshine streaming through the trees, the gardens became simply more breathtaking with every step. Rows and rows of every conceivable color of tulip (even black!) stretched like dense satin ribbons along the pathways and gently rolling hills. It was peaceful and serene, and yet at the same time, the profusion of color was more like a riot to the senses.

It seems only fitting that this quilt combines different pieced and appliquéd tulip blocks in a setting that creates a dynamic overall design as unique and spectacular as the gardens at Keukenhof.

Fabric Requirements

Yardage is based on fabrics at least 42" wide. Cut all strips selvage to selvage.

Fabric	Yards	Patches
White (background)	1⅛	48 B, 32 C, 16 F, 16 G, 8 H, 4 K
Medium scraps	1¾ total	20 A, 16 B, 32 C, 16 D, 32 E, 16 I, 8 J, 4 L 4 M, 4 N, 4 O, 8 P
Border	⅝	2 strips 4½" x 32½" 2 strips 4½" x 40½"
Backing	1⅜ or 2⅝	1 panel 44" x 44" 2 panels 23" x 44"
Binding	½	5 strips 2¼"
Batting		44" x 44"

Rotary Cutting

Measurements include seam allowance

Patch	Measurement
A	2½" x 2½"
B	1½" x 2½"
C	1½" x 1½" (see Corner-Square Technique, page 16)
D	1½" x 3½"
E–J	use patterns on pages 31–32
K	8½" x 8½"
L–P	use appliqué patterns on page 33

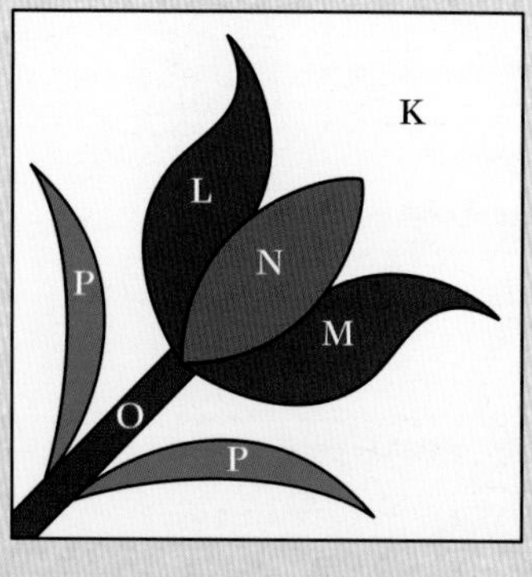

Appliqué Tulip block

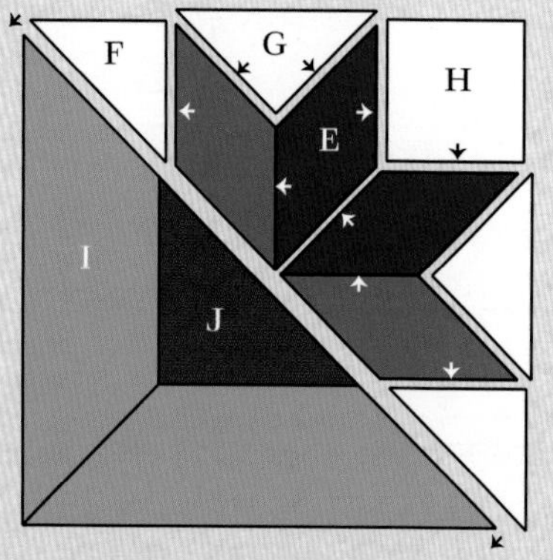

Pieced Tulip block

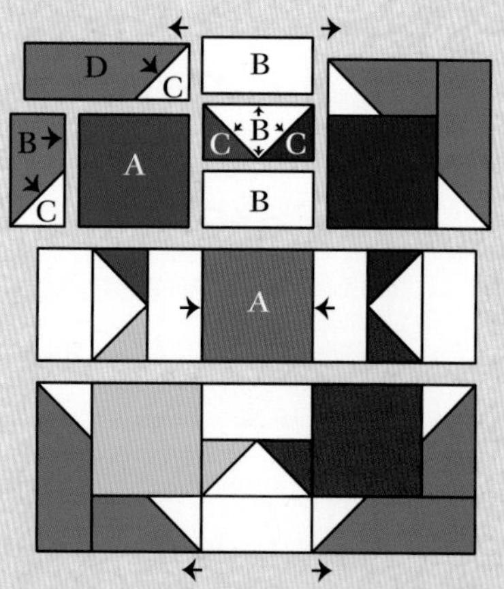

April Tulip block

Fig. 1. Block assembly

QUILT ASSEMBLY

1. As they are needed, cut the patches listed in the Fabric Requirements table. (See the Rotary Cutting table for patch measurements.)

2. Referring to the block assembly diagrams, make four Appliqué Tulip blocks, eight Pieced Tulip blocks, and four April Tulip blocks (fig. 1, page 28).

3. Arrange the blocks, as shown in the quilt assembly diagram, being careful to rotate them to achieve the desired interlocking design (fig. 2). Sew the blocks together in horizontal rows. Then join the rows.

4. Sew the side border strips to the quilt. Sew the remaining two border strips to the top and bottom of the quilt.

5. Add batting and backing then baste the layers together. Quilt as desired.

KEUKENHOF TULIPS is machine quilted, featuring a continuous tulip design on the April Tulip blocks, echo quilting on the Pieced Tulip blocks, and a crosshatch pattern on the background of the Appliquéd Tulip blocks. The border is quilted with a continuous leaf motif.

6. Use your favorite method to bind the raw edges of the quilt with the 2¼" binding strips.

FIG. 2. Quilt assembly

Hints

CORNER-SQUARE TECHNIQUE

The corner-square technique is used to add the C triangles to the B and D rectangles. See page 16 for a description of this technique.

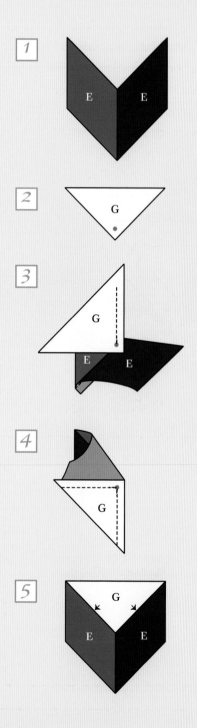

SET-IN SEAMS

When making the Pieced Tulip blocks, you will need to sew set-in seams. Don't be intimidated! Set-in seams are really quite simple to do, and they will become even easier with a bit of practice.

1. To sew an E/E/G unit, sew two diamonds (E patches) together as shown.

2. With a pencil, mark ¼" in from the corner on the wrong side of a G triangle (see red dot).

3. Align the triangle with the first diamond and sew the seam to the red dot. Use tiny stitches close to the dot to help secure the stitching. Tie off.

4. Holding the triangle and the second diamond together with your left hand, pivot the pieces so that they are aligned for the second seam. Sew the seam, starting with tiny stitches at the red dot and increasing the stitch length to normal.

5. Open the unit and press the seam allowances as shown by the arrows in the figure.

TRY THIS ...

There are many opportunities to explore the use of color and texture in this quilt. If you are unsure of how to use the traditional color wheel to find complementary colors, take your cues from nature itself. Notice all the color combinations and variations of values and hues in the flowers from your garden or growing wild alongside the highway.

Tone-on-tone prints provide a terrific way to experiment with color and design. Use a variety of textures and don't be afraid to combine fabrics you wouldn't normally consider using together in this quilt. The pieces are small enough that a funky print or unusual color won't overwhelm the other fabrics and will provide a bit of spark to your composition. Flowers in nature bloom in all kinds of interesting shades, and yet they are still beautiful. In other words, relax. Don't overanalyze your fabric choices. Be daring and have fun stretching your color comfort zone.

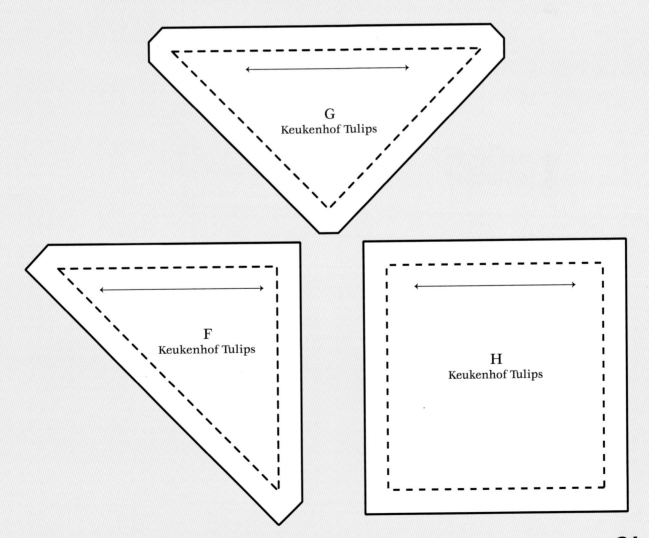

G
Keukenhof Tulips

F
Keukenhof Tulips

H
Keukenhof Tulips

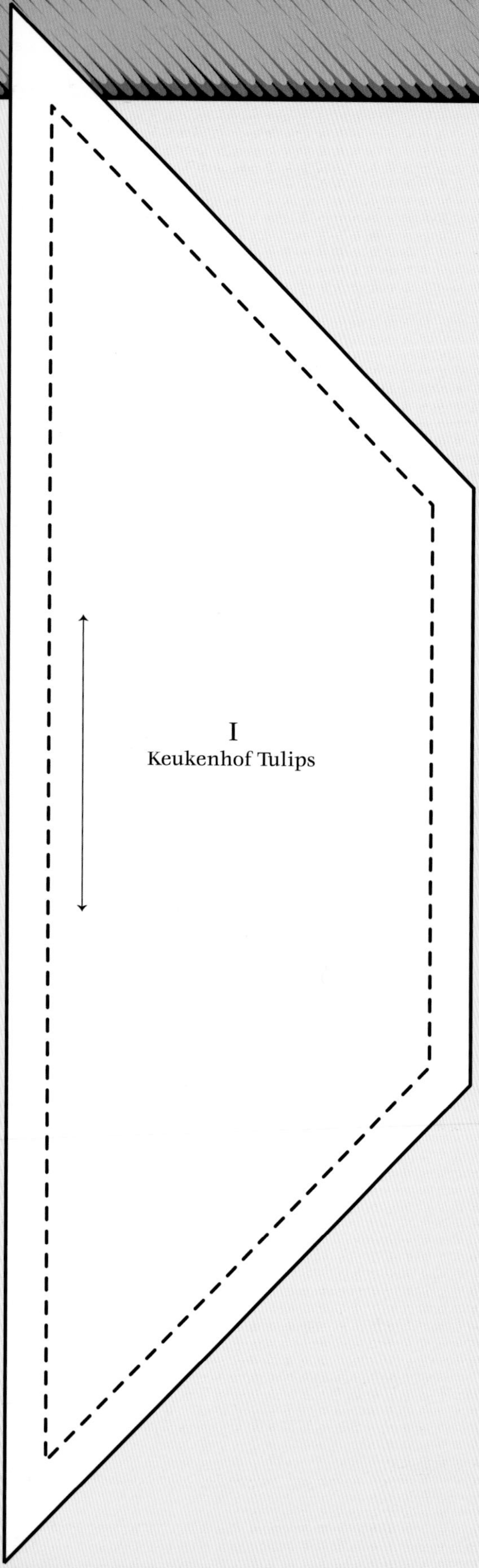

I
Keukenhof Tulips

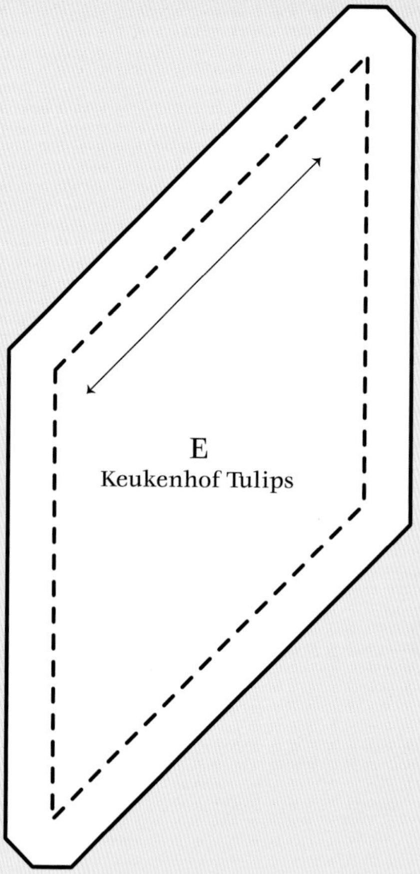

E
Keukenhof Tulips

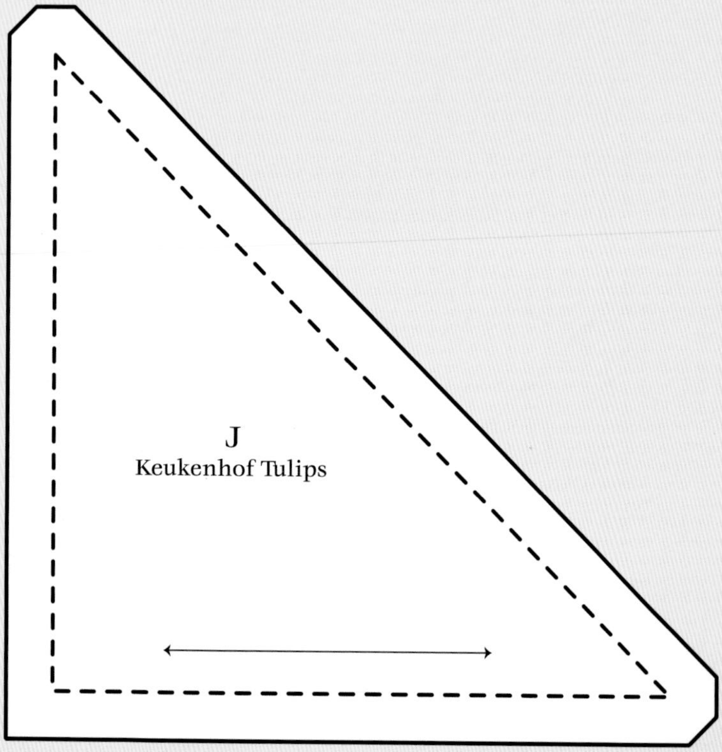

J
Keukenhof Tulips

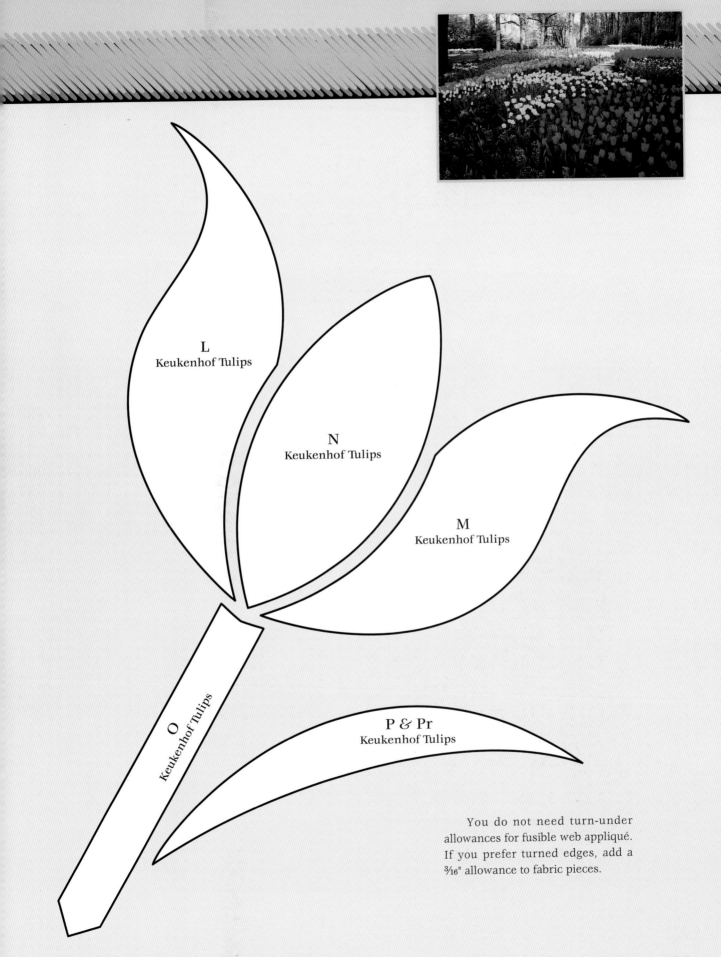

L
Keukenhof Tulips

N
Keukenhof Tulips

M
Keukenhof Tulips

O
Keukenhof Tulips

P & Pr
Keukenhof Tulips

You do not need turn-under allowances for fusible web appliqué. If you prefer turned edges, add a ³⁄₁₆" allowance to fabric pieces.

Parisian Pinwheels

PARISIAN PINWHEELS, sewn and quilted by the author

Perhaps there is no lovelier time of the year in Paris than in April. I love to stroll leisurely along the Champs Elysee, window shopping, people watching, and stopping to enjoy a freshly baked, crusty baguette and French onion soup in a quaint, sidewalk cafe. Colorful flowers overflow the window boxes, and people enjoy delicious cuisine and lively chatter. In the parks along the side streets of Paris, you'll find children playing with kites, balls, and pinwheels of all sizes and colors.

I collected small bits of traditional French Provençal fabrics to make this delightful pinwheel quilt as a happy reminder of springtime in Paris. But there's no need to worry if you can't find authentic French fabrics for your pinwheels because there are many beautiful French reproduction fabrics available right in your local quilt shop. When you get ready to make this easy-to-cut-and-piece quilt, why not stop at a local bakery first and treat yourself to a delicious, buttery croissant or baguette to enjoy while you sew. Play some French music on your CD player, and your quilt will simply fly together like a fresh spring breeze.

Fabric Requirements

Yardage is based on fabrics at least 42" wide. Cut strips selvage to selvage, except the middle and outer borders, which are cut parallel to the selvages. The border strips have extra length for mitering the corners.

FABRIC	YARDS	PATCHES
White (background and inner border)	2⅞	256 A, 24 B 2 strips 1½" x 36½" 2 strips 1½" x 48½"
Medium and dark scraps	2½ total	256 A (use at least 4 of each color) 24 B (use at least 4 each of 6 colors)
Middle border	1⅝	2 strips 3" x 41½" 2 strips 3" x 53½" (pieced)
Outer border	1⅞	2 strips 4" x 48½" (pieced) 2 strips 4" x 60½" (pieced)
Backing	3⅝	2 panels 26" x 62"
Binding	½	6 strips 2¼" x 42"
Batting		50" x 62"

ROTARY CUTTING

MEASUREMENTS INCLUDE SEAM ALLOWANCE

PATCH	MEASUREMENT
A	2⅞" x 2⅞" (cut in half diagonally)
B	4⅞" x 4⅞" (cut in half diagonally)

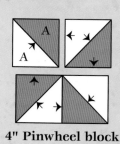

4" Pinwheel block

8" Pinwheel block

FIG. 1. Block assembly

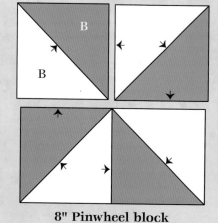

QUILT ASSEMBLY

1. From the white yardage, cut a section 48½" long and the full width of the fabric. From this section, cut the inner borders parallel to the selvages. The remainder is for the white A and B patches.

2. As they are needed, cut the patches listed in the Fabric Requirements table. (See the Rotary Cutting table for patch measurements).

3. Referring to the block assembly diagrams, make sixty-four small (4") Pinwheel blocks and six large (8") Pinwheel blocks (fig. 1).

4. Arrange the blocks in a pleasing color arrangement, then follow figure 2, page 38, to assemble the quilt top.

5. For each side of the quilt, sew the inner, middle, and outer border strips together. Treat the combined strips as a single border unit. Sew the border units to the quilt and miter the corners, being careful to match the seams at the miters.

6. Add batting and backing then baste the layers together. Quilt as desired.

PARISIAN PINWHEELS was quilted with the sewing machine's dual-feel mechanism engaged. (If your machine does not have this option, simply attach a walking foot.) No free-motion quilting was required inside the pinwheel blocks.

Begin at a block intersection along the border and sew a gentle arc in the background portion of each half-square triangle block. When you reach the other side, simply leave your needle down, pivot, and begin sewing diagonally in the other direction. The inner border features a decorative machine stitch in contrasting thread sewn through all three layers to add an extra dimension of quilting. The middle border is stitched in the ditch with invisible thread, and the outer border features a gentle meander quilting design.

7. Use your favorite method to bind the raw edges of the quilt with the 2¼" binding strips.

Hints

DECORATIVE BORDER STITCHING

The inner border provides a great opportunity to use a pretty, decorative stitch from your machine. Be bold. Try one you have never used before. Test it first on a sample quilt sandwich made from the same fabrics and batting you are using in your quilt. I stitched the decorative stitch through all three layers to add another dimension to the quilting.

LEFTOVER STRIPS

I used a beautiful, but fairly expensive, French Provençal border print for the middle border, and there were strips left over. Not wanting to waste any of this precious fabric, I decided to use the leftovers for the binding.

FIG. 2. Quilt assembly

TRY THIS ...

If you aren't ready to try free-motion quilting just yet, you can still achieve the feeling of movement on this quilt by machine quilting with continuous, gently flowing curves. This is easy to do with a walking foot or with your dual-feed mechanism engaged, if you have one. Marking the quilt top before quilting may not even be necessary. You'll love the effect because this wavy pattern creates the illusion of your pinwheels blowing in the breeze.

City of Lights

The first time I saw the Eiffel Tower was on a bitterly cold night in February. As we rode the Metro to this famous landmark, it remained hidden behind tall buildings, which housed hundreds of flats and boutiques. Then all of a sudden, we came around a corner and saw the Eiffel Tower lit up with millions of twinkling lights. The sight literally took my breath away. I will never forget that moment and the feeling of wild anticipation as we smoothly ascended to the top on an elevator. I stepped out onto the observation deck, and it seemed as if the whole world was lit up at my feet. Every light in Paris seemed to twinkle against the clear, cold, wintry night sky. It was simply a magical feeling, and now I know why Paris is called the City of Lights.

I loved making this quilt with a black background, which makes the colors sparkle and glow, just as the Eiffel Tower sparkled against that icy February night sky. Although this design appears difficult, it is actually quite easy to piece, with three simple blocks for the inner portion of the quilt and only one block cleverly rotated at different angles to make up the twinkling border. This pattern will lend itself well to using red, white, and blue fabrics, which can represent not only the colors of the French flag, but our own Stars and Stripes as well.

City of Lights

QUILT SIZE: 40" x 40"

FINISHED BLOCK SIZES: 8" x 8" and 4" x

Paris

CITY OF LIGHTS, sewn and quilted by the author

Fabric Requirements

Yardage is based on fabrics at least 42" wide. Cut all strips selvage to selvage.

FABRIC	YARDS	PATCHES
Black (background)	1⅜	96 A, 16 B, 144 C, 104 E
Yellow	½	100 C, 48 E
Light blue	¼	56 C
Lime green	¼	8 A, 44 C, 8 E
Periwinkle blue	½	24 D, 36 C
Purple	⅜	32 A, 36 C
Backing	2⅝	2 panels 23" x 44"
Binding	½	5 strips 2¼" x 42"
Batting		44" x 44"

ROTARY CUTTING
MEASUREMENTS INCLUDE SEAM ALLOWANCE

PATCH	MEASUREMENT
A	2½" x 2½"
B	2½" x 4½"
C	1½" x 1½" (see Strip Piecing 4-C Units, page 16)
D	4⅞" x 4⅞" (cut in half diagonally)
E	2⅞" x 2⅞" (cut in half diagonally)

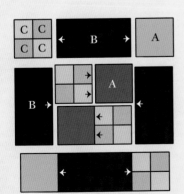

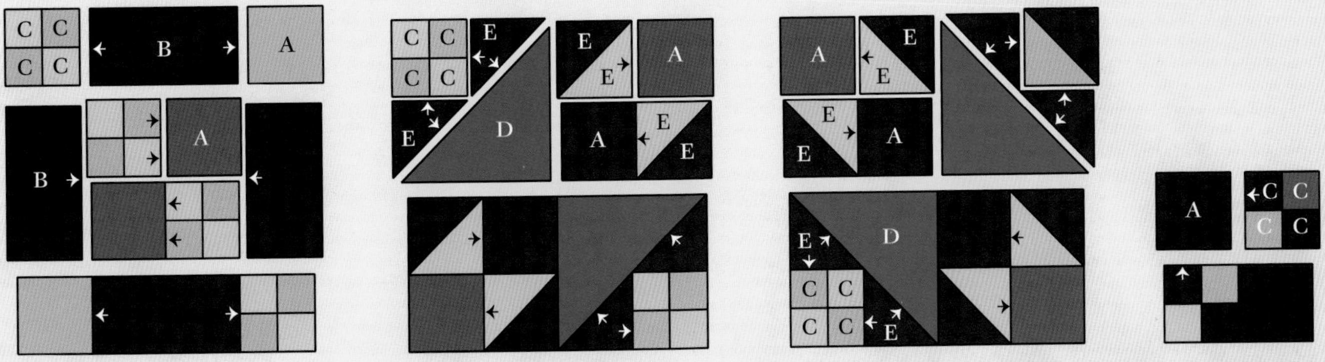

Eiffel Steps block

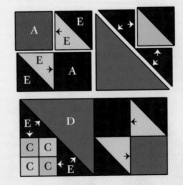

Paris Lights blocks (version A)

Paris Lights blocks (version B)

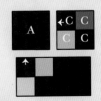

Twinkling Lights

FIG. 1. Block assembly

FIG. 2. Quilt assembly

Quilt Assembly

1. As they are needed, cut the patches listed in the Fabric Requirements table. (See the Rotary Cutting table for patch measurements.)

2. Referring to the block assembly diagrams, make four Eiffel Steps blocks, four Paris Lights blocks (version A), eight Paris Lights blocks (version B), and 36 Twinkling Lights border blocks (fig. 1, page 41).

3. Arrange the first three blocks, as shown in the quilt assembly diagram (fig. 2), being careful to rotate the blocks to achieve the desired interlocking design. Sew the blocks together in horizontal rows. Then sew the rows together.

4. Sew the Twinkling Lights border blocks together in straight rows, being careful to rotate the blocks as shown in the quilt assembly diagram. Attach these rows to the quilt, sewing the side borders first, then adding the top and bottom rows.

5. Add batting and backing then baste the layers together. Quilt as desired.

CITY OF LIGHTS was quilted in a variety of methods, including some hand quilting, machine quilting in the ditch, echo quilting, and free-motion machine quilting with variegated metallic thread and black cotton thread.

6. Use your favorite method to bind the raw edges of the quilt with the 2¼" binding strips.

City of Lights

Hints

STRIP PIECING 4-C UNITS

All the 4-C four-patch units can be strip pieced, as follows:

1. Cut 1½" strips across the appropriate fabrics. You will need a 1½" black strip for each colored strip. Sew a black and a colored strip together to make a strip-set.

2. Cut each strip-set into 1½" segments and sew two segments of different colors together to make each 4-C unit.

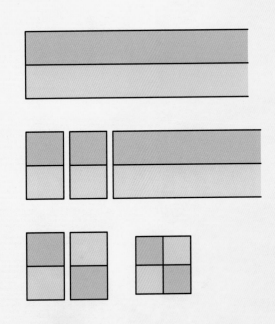

CHECK UNIT SIZE

After sewing and pressing your units, check to see that they measure 2½" before joining them into blocks. Remake any that are significantly smaller or trim any that are larger than 2½".

TRY THIS ...

If you've never embellished your quilts with metallic threads before, this is a great time to experiment. Metallic threads will add sparkle and make your quilt shimmer and shine. However, metallic threads can be brittle and break or fray easily. So, be sure to use a needle for metallic threads in your machine. You may need to loosen your upper thread tension a bit and use cotton thread that matches your backing fabric in the bobbin. Practice sewing on a sample before embellishing your quilt, and don't be afraid to use different colors of metallic or variegated colors on the same quilt.

Market Day

MARKET DAY, sewn, machine embroidered, and
machine quilted by the author

Travel through the German countryside on a Saturday and you'll most likely find an outdoor market in the center of every village and small town. The merchants and farmers at these markets sell all kinds of fresh fruits, vegetables, cheeses, meats, spices, eggs, and even honey from local hives. I've bartered for asparagus, sampled sweet strawberries, and bought heads of lettuce so large and leafy that they looked like beautiful table centerpieces. According to local residents, it's customary to shop in the market by carrying your own basket for the vendors to fill with your purchases. Plastic or paper bags are so "out of place." Besides, in keeping with the quilters' tradition of recycling, baskets are much more Earth friendly.

This quilt features the traditional Corn and Beans block, stitched in four mouth-watering colors and embellished with nine machine-embroidered vegetable blocks. As you piece this quilt, use your imagination and think of all the tasty treats you could fill your basket with on market day.

Fabric Requirements

Yardage is based on fabrics at least 42" wide. Cut all strips selvage to selvage.

FABRIC	YARDS	PATCHES
Black	2⅞	160 B, 480 D, 9 E
Green	⅝	12 A, 48 C, 48 D
Orange	⅝	12 A, 48 C, 48 D
Purple	½	8 A, 32 C, 32 D
Yellow	½	8 A, 32 C, 32 D
Multicolor print border	1½	2 strips 6½" x 53" (pieced)
		2 strips 6½" x 65" (pieced)
Backing	4⅛	2 panels 35" x 69"
Binding	⅝	7 strips 2¼" x 42"
Batting		69" x 69"

ROTARY CUTTING
MEASUREMENTS INCLUDE SEAM ALLOWANCE

PATCH	MEASUREMENT
A	2" x 2"
B	2" x 3½"
C	3⅞" x 3⅞" (cut in half diagonally)
D	2⅜" x 2⅜" (cut in half diagonally)
E	9½" x 9½" (trim to 8" x 8" after embroidering)

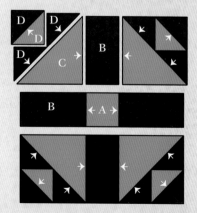

FIG. 1. Corn and Beans block assembly

Quilt A TRAVEL SOUVENIR *Kimberly Einmo*

QUILT ASSEMBLY

1. As they are needed, cut the patches listed in the Fabric Requirements table. (See the Rotary Cutting table for patch measurements.)

2. Referring to the block assembly diagram, make twelve green, twelve orange, eight purple, and eight yellow Corn and Beans blocks (fig. 1, page 46).

3. Machine embroider the nine E squares, if desired, then trim them to 8" x 8".

4. Arrange the Corn and Beans blocks and the embroidered blocks in the order shown in the quilt assembly diagram (fig. 2, page 48). Sew the blocks together in rows then join the rows.

5. Sew the side border strips to the quilt then add the top and bottom strips.

6. Add batting and backing then baste the layers together. Quilt as desired.

MARKET DAY was machine quilted by stitching in the ditch around each of the blocks, with invisible thread in the top and a 40-weight cotton thread (matching the backing fabric) in the bobbin. The wide outer border features a large, meandering, stipple stitch sewn in a variegated 30-weight cotton thread.

7. Use your favorite method to bind the raw edges of the quilt with the 2¼" binding strips.

Hints

BINDING SUGGESTION

I had leftover strips from the four medium colors used in the Corn and Beans blocks. So I trimmed them to 2¼" x 18" and pieced them together, end to end, alternating the colors for a fun, eye-catching binding.

EMBROIDERY

For my embroidery, I used the Pfaff Creative #301 Garden Memory Card, designs 2, 4, 5, 6, 7, 9, 12, 13, and 16.

TRY THIS ...

If you don't have a computerized embroidery machine, or if you want a fast and fun alternative to the embroidered blocks, you could simply use 8" x 8" squares cut from a novelty print as the featured E pieces. There may be a number of fruit and vegetable print fabrics available at your local quilt shop that would look simply delicious in place of the machine-embroidered vegetable squares.

FIG. 2. Quilt assembly

Memories of Germany

The Rheinland Pfalz Quilt Guild, where I was a member at Ramstein Air Base, Germany, offered a quilt challenge entitled Memories of Germany. The rules were simple. Participants were provided with a beautiful fat quarter of purple grapes and green leaves. It was to be included in a quilted wallhanging designed with personal memories of living in this wonderful country. I was instantly inspired. I pieced star blocks from the challenge fabric, and appliquéd pretzels, grapes, and an edelweiss appliqué I had purchased in Bavaria in the center of the quilt. I machine embroidered a castle, flower basket, wine bottle, and nutcracker in the corner blocks. Because we lived in the region that is well known for its vineyards along the Mosel and Rhein Rivers, grapes, leaves, and a vine seemed the perfect choice for the border.

There was just one perplexing problem. I wanted to include an easily recognizable blue autobahn sign on the quilt, but the bright blue color of the sign certainly didn't lend itself to the purple and green color scheme. My solution? I traced a picture of the sign and appliquéd the fabrics on the back as a quilt label instead. I was thrilled when my quilt won first place.

QUILT SIZE: 37" x 37"

FINISHED BLOCK SIZES: 12" x 12"

MEMORIES OF GERMANY, sewn, machine embroidered, and hand quilted by the author

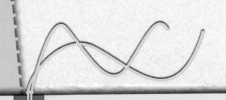

Fabric Requirements

Yardage is based on fabrics at least 42" wide. Cut all strips selvage to selvage.

FABRIC	YARDS	PATCHES
Off white (background and outer border)	1¼	16 B, 16 D 4 strips 5½" x 27½"
Grape print	¼	2 A, 16 C
Medium purple	¼	4 C
Dark purple	¼	4 C
Light green 1	¼	4 C, 6 leaves (pattern 6)
Light green 2	⅜	1 A, 8 C, 6 leaves (pattern 6)
Middle green	¼	1 A, 8 C
Dark green	⅜	4 C, 8 leaves (pattern 6)
Purple (inner border)	⅜	4 strips 2" x 24½"
Light green 3 (corner squares)	⅜	4 E
Purple scraps	⅛ total	104 grapes (pattern 7)
Brown	⅝	4 pretzels (pattern 4 and 5) 1 square 18" x 18" (bias vine)
White	scrap	1 edelweiss (patterns 1–10)
Yellow	scrap	1 edelweiss center (patterns 11–17)
Backing	1¼	1 panel 41" x 41"
Binding	⅜	5 strips 2½" x 42"
Batting		44" x 44"

ROTARY CUTTING
MEASUREMENTS INCLUDE SEAM ALLOWANCE

PATCH	MEASUREMENT
A	4¾" x 4¾"
B	7¼" x 7¼" (cut in quarters diagonally)
C	3⅞" x 3⅞" (cut in half diagonally)
D	3½" x 3½"
E	7" x 7"
Appliques	use patterns on pages 54–56

Additional Supplies

White embroidery floss
Light- or medium-weight fusible web
¼" dark-brown fusible bias tape, 5½ yd. roll
Glue stick
Double machine needle, size: 4.0/100

QUILT ASSEMBLY

1. As they are needed, cut the patches listed in the Fabric Requirements table. (See the Rotary Cutting table for patch measurements.)

2. Referring to the quilt photo and the block assembly diagram, make four Germany Star blocks in the color combinations shown (fig. 1).

3. Machine embroider the four border corner (E) squares with your chosen designs.

4. Arrange the blocks as shown in the quilt assembly diagram (fig. 2, page 53). Sew the blocks together in horizontal rows. Then join the rows.

5. Sew an inner border strip to each of the four sides of the quilt and miter the corners.

6. Sew the side outer border strips to the quilt. Add the E corner squares to the remaining two border strips then sew them to the top and bottom of the quilt.

ADDING APPLIQUES

1. Following the directions on page 17, prepare all the appliqués for fusing.

2. Using a hot iron, fuse edelweiss pieces to the background in numerical order. Cover the raw edges and add petal details with either a machine satin stitch or hand embroidery stitch.

3. Use the 18" brown square to make a ⅜" wide continuous bias tube 150" long, as described on page 18. (The cut width of the strips is 1¼".)

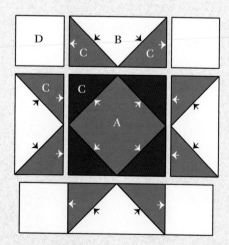

FIG. 1. Block assembly

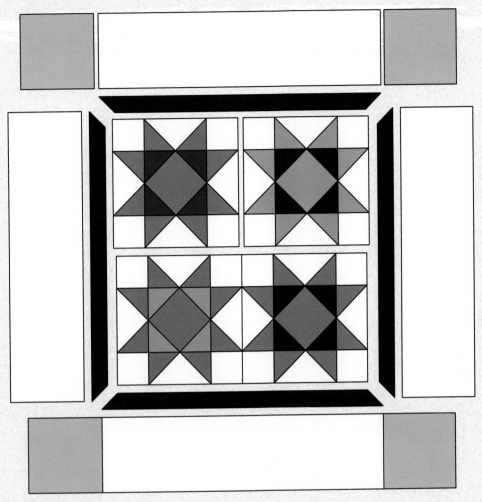

FIG. 2. Quilt assembly

4. Use a glue stick and straight pins to curve sections of the ⅜" bias strip into four pretzel shapes (page 54). Pin the shapes to the quilt and finish the edges with machine or hand stitching.

5. If desired, add tiny white or clear seed beads to the pretzels to give the appearance of salt crystals.

6. Lightly trace the border pattern (pages 55–56) on all four outer borders. Peel the paper backing from the ¼" fusible bias tape. Following the traced lines, press the ⅜" brown bias tube in place. Machine stitch the bias tape with a double machine needle and matching thread.

7. Fuse the leaf shapes and grapes to the border as shown in the quilt assembly diagram. Finish the appliqué edges with machine or hand stitching.

8. Embroider the veins in the leaves by hand, using two strands of embroidery floss.

Finishing

1. Add batting and backing then baste the layers together. Quilt as desired.

I hand quilted the top with outlines of the leaf appliqués in the open white spaces and simple diagonal lines spaced 2½" apart in the outer borders. I added curlicues around the edelweiss in the center, simple outline quilting inside and outside the pretzel appliqués, and a cable design in the inner border.

2. Use your favorite method to bind the raw edges of the quilt with the 2¼" binding strips.

Hint

EMBROIDERY DESIGNS

I used the Blumen Basket from Pfaff Creative Fantasy Card #15 Mother's Day, Cactus Punch designs for Small Prince #SIG11013 and Magical Castle #SIG25006, and the Wine Bottle and Glass design from Embroidery Library.

TRY THIS ...

Embellish and personalize this quilt to make it truly your own. Begin with the basic pattern, which comprises four star blocks and simple borders with corner squares. You may choose to appliqué a different flower in the quilt center. In place of the machine embroidery, you could simply use squares of your featured print fabric or add additional grape or leaf appliqués in the corner blocks. Instead of grapes in the border, consider adding appliqué seashells, snowflakes, autumn leaves, or sports motifs. Embroider designs that remind you of your vacation or use photo transfers in the border corner blocks. Add trinkets and charms. Be creative and most of all have fun!

You do not need turn-under allowances for fusible web appliqué. If you prefer turned edges, add a ³⁄₁₆" allowance to fabric pieces.

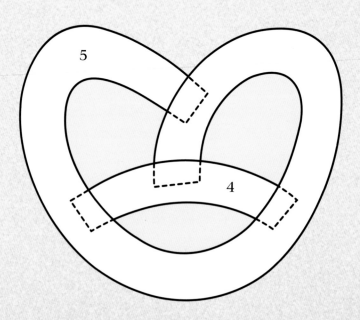

5

2

1

4

12

11

6

13

17

16

3

15

14

7

10

8

9

You do not need turn-under allowances for fusible web appliqué. If you prefer turned edges, add a ³⁄₁₆" allowance to fabric pieces.

leaf
6

grapes
7

center of
border

leaf
6

Memories of Germany

leaf
6

grapes
6

Mitered corner

You do not need turn-under allowances for fusible web appliqué. If you prefer turned edges, add a 3/16" allowance to fabric pieces.

The city of Karlovy Vary lies in the Czech Republic, about two hours from Prague. It is a brilliant jewel tucked discretely away in a beautiful, wooded valley with the crystal clear Tepla River running through the heart of town. This centuries-old city is well known to Europeans for its reported healing waters, which flow from deep, natural sulfur springs in the center of town.

Serious shoppers know Karlovy Vary for its spectacular buys on items such as lace, locally mined garnets, and exquisite diamond-cut Bohemian crystal. Highly sought after for its clarity and affordability, Bohemian crystal is recognizable for a multi-faceted star design, which is evident on most of the crystal pieces. Many shops line the streets with gleaming crystal chandeliers hanging in the windows, and inside, you'll find store shelves lined with vases, stemware, decanters, bowls, and crystal figurines of every shape and size.

I designed this quilt to reflect that distinctive, recognizable star pattern and to capture the loveliness of a city once hidden behind the Iron Curtain. Now, Karlovy Vary is a sparkling gem with a brilliant future in the European community.

Bohemian Crystal

Bohemian Crystal

BOHEMIAN CRYSTAL, sewn and machine quilted by the author

Fabric Requirements

Yardage is based on fabrics at least 42" wide. Cut all strips selvage to selvage.

FABRIC	YARDS	PATCHES
Tan (background)	1⅛	120 A, 24 B, 20 C, 32 E
Teal	½	144 A
Rust (includes accent strips)	½	24 A, 24 B
		4 strips 1" x 39½"
Purple (includes inner border)	⅝	32 D, 32 Dr
		2 strips 2" x 36½"
		2 strips 2" x 39½"
Floral (outer border)	½	4 strips 3½" x 39½"
Backing	3	2 panels 25¼" x 50"
Binding	½	5 strips 2¼" x 42"
Batting		50" x 50"

ROTARY CUTTING

MEASUREMENTS INCLUDE SEAM ALLOWANCE

PATCH	MEASUREMENT
A	2" x 2" (see Strip Piecing Four-Patches, page 16)
B	3⅞" x 3⅞" (cut in half diagonally)
C	3½" x 3½"
D/Dr	use pattern on page 61
E	use pattern on page 61

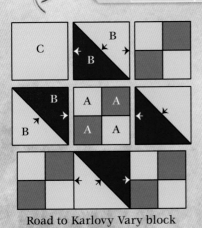

Road to Karlovy Vary block

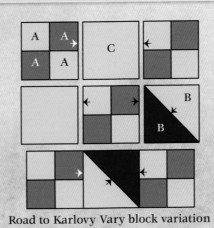

Road to Karlovy Vary block variation

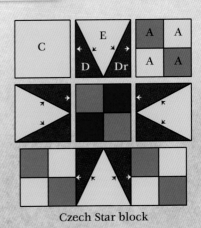

Czech Star block

FIG. 1. Block and four-patch assembly

Quilt Assembly

1. As they are needed, cut the patches listed in the Fabric Requirements table. (See the Rotary Cutting table, page 59, for the patch measurements.)

2. Referring to the block assembly diagrams (fig. 1, page 59), make four Road to Karlovy Vary blocks, four Road to Karlovy Vary block variations, and eight Czech Star blocks. You will also need four blue and rust four-patch units for the corner squares in the outer border.

3. Arrange the blocks as shown in the quilt assembly diagram, being careful to rotate them to achieve the desired interlocking design (fig. 2). Sew the blocks together in horizontal rows then sew the rows together.

4. Sew the side inner border strips to the quilt then add the top and bottom inner border strips.

5. To add accent strips, fold the 1" rust strips in half, wrong sides together. Match the raw edges and machine baste the folded strips to the inner border strips with a ⅛" seam allowance.

6. Sew the side outer border strips to the quilt, being careful to leave the accent strips facing the inner border.

7. Sew a four-patch unit to each end of the remaining two outer border strips. Add these strips to the top and bottom of the quilt.

8. Add batting and backing then baste the layers together. Quilt as desired.

BOHEMIAN CRYSTAL is machine quilted with matching thread on the background fabric. A diamond grid was drawn in 2" widths, and the diamonds were filled with stipple quilting. The purple and rust triangles are stitched in the ditch to provide extra definition for the star points. The inner border features a decorative machine stitch with a contrasting thread that is stitched through all three layers for added dimension. The outer border has a continuous triple-cable design, sewn in the same color thread as the stippling in the quilt center.

9. Use your favorite method to bind the raw edges of the quilt with the 2¼" binding strips.

FIG. 2. Quilt assembly

Hint

STRIP PIECING FOUR-PATCHES

The four-patch (4-A) units for the blocks can be strip pieced as follows:

1. Cut the following 2" strips: five tan, six teal, and one rust. Sew a tan strip to each teal strip. Sew the remaining teal strip to the rust strip. You will have a total of six strip-sets.

2. Cut each strip-set into 2" segments and sew two segments together as shown to make each four-patch unit. Set aside four teal and rust four-patches for the outer border.

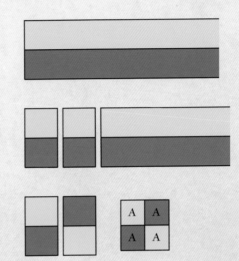

TRY THIS ...

Would you like to learn the secret to perfect points in the center of your four-patch units? Place the units right sides together and feed the patches underneath the presser foot with the raw edge of the exposed seam facing the presser foot, instead of away from it. This gently pushes the seams to "snuggle" together so they form a sharp point where they intersect.

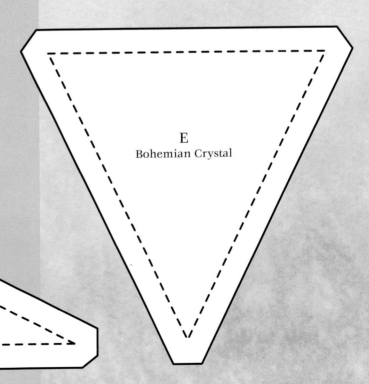

D & Dr
Bohemian Crystal

E
Bohemian Crystal

QUILT SIZE: 60" x 60"

FINISHED BLOCK SIZE: 10" x 10"

Notting Hill Hidden Garden

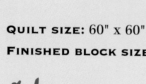

NOTTING HILL HIDDEN GARDEN, sewn and machine quilted by the author

*J*ust before we moved overseas, my husband and I saw the movie "Notting Hill," and because we are romantics at heart, it instantly became one of our favorite films. So, once we got settled, one of our first trips was to London, and we just had to visit Portobello Road and Notting Hill. We hoped to catch a glimpse of that famous "blue door" featured in the movie as the home of Hugh Grant's character, William Thacker. Try as we might, we never did locate that door. Then we heard from some friendly local chaps that the new owners of the house had painted the door black!

One day, we stumbled on a garden hidden behind iron gates and thick hedges. Inside, the flowers, plants, and trees were lush, fragrant, and meticulously groomed. I was amazed at the profusion of red geraniums, which were everywhere. So this quilt is a tribute to those small properties of paradise hidden quietly all over London.

Fabric Requirements

Yardage is based on fabrics at least 42" wide. Cut all strips selvage to selvage, except the outer border.

FABRIC	YARDS	PATCHES
White (includes sashing)	⅞	64 B, 24 C
Red	½	64 B
Green 1 (block centers)	⅛	16 B
Green 2	¾	64 A
Blue (includes inner border)	⅝	9 B
		2 strips 2½" x 46½" (pieced)
		2 strips 2½" x 50½" (pieced)
Floral (includes outer border)	2⅜	64 A
		2 strips 5½" x 50½" (cut parallel to selvages)
		2 strips 5½" x 60½" (cut parallel to selvages)
Backing	3¾	2 panels 33" x 64"
Binding	⅝	7 strips 2¼" x 42"
Batting		64" x 64"

ROTARY CUTTING

MEASUREMENTS INCLUDE SEAM ALLOWANCE

PATCH	MEASUREMENT
A	4⅞" x 4⅞" (cut in half diagonally)
B	2½" x 2½"
C	2½ x 10½"

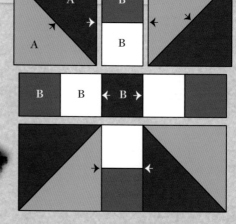

FIG. 1. Notting Hill block assembly

FIG. 2. Quilt assembly

Quilt Assembly

1. Cut the inner border and outer border strips lengthwise along the fabric before cutting the patches.

2. As they are needed, cut the patches listed in the Fabric Requirements table. (See the Rotary Cutting table for patch measurements.)

3. Referring to the block assembly diagram, make sixteen Notting Hill blocks (fig. 1).

4. Arrange the blocks, sashing strips (C pieces), and cornerstones (blue B pieces) as shown in the quilt assembly diagram (fig. 2). Sew the blocks, sashing pieces, and cornerstones in rows. Then join the rows.

5. Sew the side inner border strips to the quilt. Then add the top and bottom inner border strips. Repeat for the outer border strips.

6. Add batting and backing then baste the layers together. Quilt as desired.

This quilt is machine quilted very simply, with white thread, in the ditch around each of the patches and diagonally through the block centers. A decorative floral stitch enhances the inner border, and a continuous cable design is machine quilted in the outer border.

7. Use your favorite method to bind the raw edges of the quilt with the 2¼" binding strips.

Notting Hill Hidden Garden

Hint

DECORATIVE MACHINE STITCHING

The inner border provides a great opportunity to use a pretty, decorative machine stitch. Be bold. Try one you have never used before. Just be sure to test it on a sample quilt sandwich made with the same fabrics, batting, and thread you plan to use in your quilt. I quilted the decorative stitch through all three layers to add another dimension of quilting.

TRY THIS ...

I fell in love with the red and green geranium print fabric. My personal challenge was to create a quilt that didn't look like a Christmas quilt. I used colors from the floral print, plus a splash of royal blue as an accent that makes the quilt look summery and fresh.

This is such a simple quilt to piece, why not select fabrics you might not normally choose? If you prefer soft muted colors, try using a bold combination of bright batiks. If you usually sew with clear jewel tones, try a sampling of the yummy 1930s' reproduction prints. Be daring and teach yourself to use complementary colors from the color wheel and make a bold departure from your current color comfort zone.

English Estate

A short train ride from the hustle and bustle of London, you will find some of the loveliest manors and sprawling estates dotting the gently rolling English countryside. Built in a bygone era, these magnificent homes are maintained today in all their stately glory and elegance. Estate grounds host mirrored pools with sparkling fountains, extensive gardens, and ornately carved gazebos. Some gardens have elaborate mazes of twisting cobbled pathways lined with tall, thick hedges. Gleaming white arbors covered with rose blossoms as thick as velvet lend an air of romance straight from a Jane Austin novel. Their fragrance is as heady as love itself. The pace is slow, and every moment in this setting is meant to be savored.

So it is with this stunning quilt. Three traditional quilt blocks with British heritage names combine in a unique setting to create a secondary design as intricate as a garden hedge maze. However, it is not difficult to piece. Just relax and take your time as you sew. Thoroughly savor the slower pace of assembling this quilt piece-by-piece, block-by-block.

English Estate

ENGLISH ESTATE, sewn by Mary Flynn, RAF Lakenheath, England, and machine quilted by Carolyn Archer, Lebanon, Ohio

Fabric Requirements

Yardage is based on fabrics at least 42" wide. Cut all strips selvage to selvage, except the outer border.

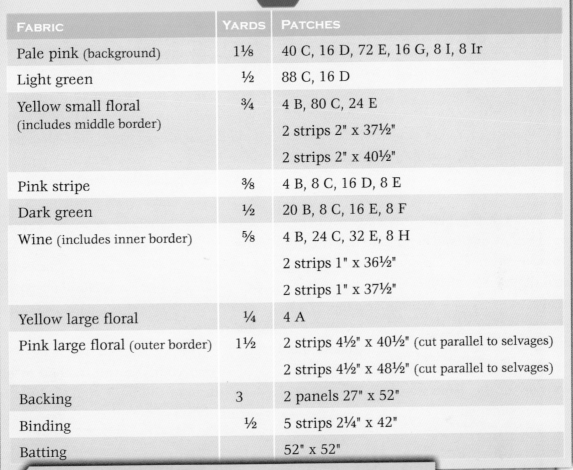

FABRIC	YARDS	PATCHES
Pale pink (background)	1⅛	40 C, 16 D, 72 E, 16 G, 8 I, 8 Ir
Light green	½	88 C, 16 D
Yellow small floral (includes middle border)	¾	4 B, 80 C, 24 E
		2 strips 2" x 37½"
		2 strips 2" x 40½"
Pink stripe	⅜	4 B, 8 C, 16 D, 8 E
Dark green	½	20 B, 8 C, 16 E, 8 F
Wine (includes inner border)	⅝	4 B, 24 C, 32 E, 8 H
		2 strips 1" x 36½"
		2 strips 1" x 37½"
Yellow large floral	¼	4 A
Pink large floral (outer border)	1½	2 strips 4½" x 40½" (cut parallel to selvages)
		2 strips 4½" x 48½" (cut parallel to selvages)
Backing	3	2 panels 27" x 52"
Binding	½	5 strips 2¼" x 42"
Batting		52" x 52"

ROTARY CUTTING
MEASUREMENTS INCLUDE SEAM ALLOWANCE

PATCH	MEASUREMENT
A	4¾" x 4¾"
B	3⅞" x 3⅞" (cut in half diagonally)
C	2⅜" x 2⅜" (cut in half diagonally)
D	2" x 3½" (see Corner-Square Technique, page 16)
E	2" x 2" (see Corner-Square Technique, page 16)
F	3½" x 3½"
G	5⅜" x 5⅜" (cut in half diagonally)
H	1⅜" x 6" (see Hints: Quick H Stems, page 71)
I/Ir	4⅞" x 4⅞" (see Hints: Quick I/Ir Triangles, page 72)

Quilt Assembly

1. As needed, cut the patches listed in the Fabric Requirements table. (See the Rotary Cutting table, page 69), for patch measurements.)

2. Referring to the block assembly diagrams, make four King's Crown blocks, eight English Ivy blocks, and four English Clover blocks (fig. 1).

3. Arrange the blocks as shown in the quilt assembly diagram, being careful to rotate the blocks to achieve the desired interlocking design (fig. 2). Sew the blocks together in horizontal rows. Then sew the rows together.

4. Sew the side inner border strips to the quilt. Then add the top and bottom inner border strips. In the same way, add the middle and outer border strips.

5. Add batting and backing then baste the layers together. Quilt as desired.

ENGLISH ESTATE *is machine quilted (on a long-arm quilting machine) with a combination of ecru and invisible threads. The King's Crown and English Clover blocks are both quilted with a rose and leaf wreath design. The English Ivy blocks are quilted with floral and leaf highlights to give the flower in the block more definition. Each of the burgundy stems contains a curved line of stitching, and the light backgrounds are stipple quilted closely together. The inner border echoes the gently curving line of the flower stems, and the outer border is quilted with continuous-line rose blossoms and leaves.*

6. Use your favorite method to bind the raw edges of the quilt with the 2¼" binding strips.

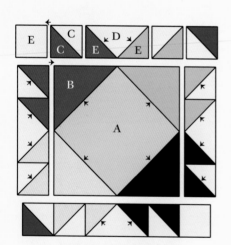

King's Crown block

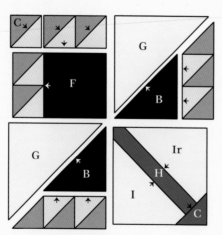

English Ivy block

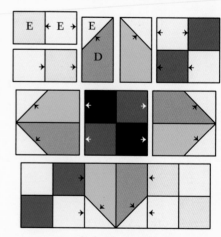

English Clover block

FIG. 1. Block assembly

FIG. 2. Quilt assembly

Hints

QUICK H STEMS

To make an English Ivy stem (patch H) quickly and without having to use a template, fold a 1⅜" x 6" strip in half lengthwise and use the 45-degree angle on your ruler to cut off the end as shown.

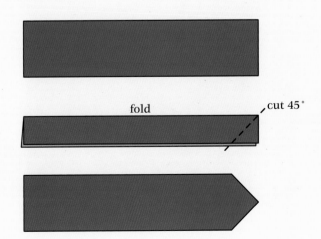

fold   cut 45°

English Estate

QUICK I/IR TRIANGLES

To make the two background triangles on either side of the stem, place two I squares right sides together and cut through both diagonally, corner to corner, to make two pairs of triangles. Lay template I/Ir (page 73) on top of one pair and cut the angle. The result will be an I and an Ir patch. Repeat for the second pair of triangles.

QUICK E/D UNITS

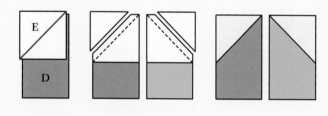

Draw a diagonal line, corner to corner, on the wrong side of an E square. Place the square on top of a D rectangle as shown. Sew on the line. Trim off the extra fabric leaving a ¼" seam allowance, then press open. Be sure to follow the diagrams carefully to make the two mirror-image units.

TRY THIS ...

Now is the perfect time to improve your free-motion machine quilting skills. Try marking the outer border with an easy continuous quilting motif, such as a heart, flower, or geometric design. The quilt is small enough that there won't be too much drag as you move it around beneath the needle. If you use a busy print fabric in the outer border, the print will help to hide any less-than-perfect stitches. As you gain confidence in using this technique, you will soon be ready to tackle bigger quilts and more intricate quilting designs.

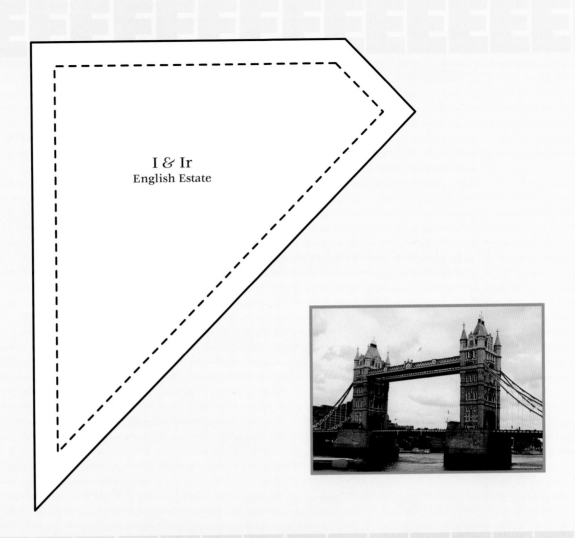

I & Ir
English Estate

English Estate variation

Take a vacation to paradise by simply changing the fabrics and colors for English Estate (page 68). The tropical hues in this version (shown on page 4) are reminiscent of white sandy beaches, fresh pineapples, and swaying palm trees. The traditional blocks go "Hawaiian" with a touch of Asian influence in this version. Aloha!

QUILT SIZE: 66" x 66"

FINISHED BLOCK SIZES: 9" x 9"

Trip to Dublin

TRIP TO DUBLIN, sewn by Judy Schrader, Bann, Germany,
and machine quilted by Carolyn Archer, Lebanon, Ohio

Ireland has a charm and a sparkling bit of magic all its own. The lush countryside is perpetually green, yet the hillsides are speckled with rocks and stones. The air is fresh, misty, and clean, and the villages are so captivating that the rest of the world seems far away. It might be the Irish people themselves who make a trip to Ireland so enchanting. Who can resist listening to their lilting accents and lively stories down at the corner pub? There is plenty to see and do and plenty not to do if you so choose… just relax and enjoy the local scenery.

This quilt combines variations of two traditional blocks, the Irish Chain and Dublin Steps. With a few clever fabric placements within the blocks, they combine to create a delightful pattern reminiscent of a Trip Around the World design. Sewing the blocks is fast and easy, and with a little luck 'o the Irish, you'll be finished in no time at all.

Fabric Requirements

Yardage is based on fabrics at least 42" wide. Cut all strips selvage to selvage.

FABRIC	YARDS	PATCHES
Off-white (background)	1¾	92 A, 36 B, 64 C, 72 D
Light green	¾	216 B
Yellow scraps	⅝ total	64 C
Dark green	½	36 B, 72 D
Gold scraps	⅜ total	24 A
Brown scraps	¾ total	216 B
Inner border	¾	2 strips 2½" x 54½" (pieced)
		2 strips 2½" x 58½" (pieced)
Outer border	1⅛	2 strips 4½" x 58½" (pieced)
		2 strips 4½" x 66½" (pieced)
Backing	4	2 panels 36" x 70"
Binding	⅝	7 strips 2¼" x 42"
Batting		70" x 70"

ROTARY CUTTING

MEASUREMENTS INCLUDE SEAM ALLOWANCE

PATCH	MEASUREMENT
A	3½" x 3½"
B	2" x 2"
C	3⅞" x 3⅞" (cut in half diagonally)
D	2⅜" x 2⅜" (cut in half diagonally)

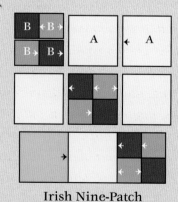

Irish Nine-Patch

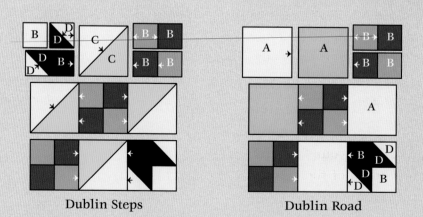

Dublin Steps   Dublin Road

FIG. 1. Block assembly

QUILT ASSEMBLY

1. As they are needed, cut the patches listed in the Fabric Requirements table. (See the Rotary Cutting table for patch measurements.)

2. Referring to the block assembly diagrams, make sixteen Irish Nine Patch blocks, sixteen Dublin Steps blocks, and four Dublin Road blocks (fig. 1).

3. Arrange the blocks, as shown in the quilt assembly diagram, being careful to rotate them to achieve the desired interlocking design (fig. 2). Sew the blocks together in horizontal rows. Then sew the rows together.

4. Sew the side border strips to the quilt. Sew the remaining two border strips to the top and bottom of the quilt. Add the outer border in the same way.

5. Add batting and backing then baste the layers together. Quilt as desired.

Trip to Dublin is quilted with a variety of machine quilting designs. The same ecru thread is used throughout for continuity. The Irish Chain blocks feature an easy curved cross, which appears to link the chains together. The pieced tulip design is carried through to the background blocks with more quilting, and the green pieced tulip points are echo-quilted ¼" inside the lines. The inner and outer borders feature two different continuous leaf patterns, which vary in size and texture.

6. Use your favorite method to bind the raw edges of the quilt with the 2¼" binding strips.

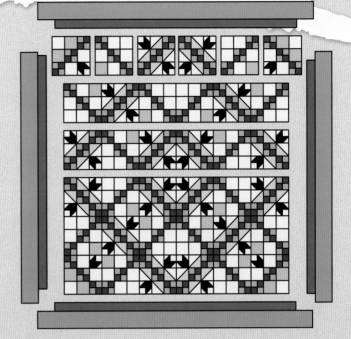

FIG. 2. Quilt assembly

TRY THIS ...

This is a great quilt for using fat quarters and pieces of fabric that are too large to be put into your scrap basket yet too small to go back into your stash. Group your fabrics together by color before cutting, and arrange them randomly in the blocks, paying attention only to the color placement. This planned scrappy effect will add sparkle to your quilt and will allow you to use small bits of leftover fabric that are too wonderful to discard.

QUILT SIZE: 50" x 50"

FINISHED BLOCK SIZES: 9" x 9"

Chocolate and Lace

CHOCOLATE AND LACE, sewn by Carla Conner, Ramstein, Germany, and machine
quilted by Carolyn Archer, Lebanon, Ohio. The lace doilies were purchased in Belgium

$\mathcal{B}$ elgium has so much to offer. There are modern, bustling cities filled with culture and art, and charming villages that look as if they were lost in time. The people are friendly and immensely proud of their traditions... and their food. Belgian cuisine is some of the finest in the world, and the regional specialties include golden Belgian waffles; fluffy egg omelets; and paper-thin, delectable crepes dusted with the finest of sugars. There are many things to appreciate about this country, not the least of which is chocolate. Perhaps no chocolate on earth is as sinfully rich and decadent as Belgian chocolate.

Belgians take great pride in the heritage of their beautiful tapestries and exquisite handmade lace, which is of the finest quality and second to none. It seemed only fitting to combine two of my favorite things in a quilt: delicate Belgian lace and luscious chocolate brown. I also included rich peach and delicious pink fabrics that look as if they would simply melt in your mouth, just like that world-renowned chocolate.

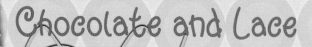

Fabric Requirements

Yardage is based on fabrics at least 42" wide. Cut all strips selvage to selvage. Border measurements are extra long to aid in mitering the corners.

Chocolate and Lace

FABRIC	YARDS	PATCHES
Light pink (background)	1¼	32 B, 8 C, 64 D, 16 E, 24 F, 8 H, 8 Hr, 8 J
Light peach 1	¼	8 C, 16 D, 8 E
Light peach 2	¼	8 C, 16 D, 8 E
Multicolor	⅛	8 A
Pink	⅛	8 F
Dark brown	⅜	16 C, 32 D
Basket brown	⅜	16 E, 32 G, 8 I
Basket peach	⅜	24 E, 8 D
Inner border	⅝	4 strips 2½" x 42"
Outer border	1¾	4 strips 5½" x 52½" (cut parallel to selvages)
Backing	3¼	2 panels 28" x 55"
Binding	½	6 strips 2¼" x 42"
Batting		54" x 54"

ROTARY CUTTING
MEASUREMENTS INCLUDE SEAM ALLOWANCE

PATCH	MEASUREMENT
A	3½" x 3½"
B	3" x 3" (cut in half diagonally)
C	3⅞" x 3⅞" (cut in half diagonally)
D	2⅜" x 2⅜" (cut in half diagonally)
E	2" x 2"
F	2" x 3½"
G	3⅜" x 3⅜" (cut in quarters diagonally)
H/Hr	2" x 6⅞" (see Hints, Quick H/Hr Patches, page 82)
I	1½" x 5½" (see Hints, Quick I Patches, page 82)
J	9⅞" x 9⅞" (cut in half diagonally)

Quilt A TRAVEL SOUVENIR *Kimberly Einmo*

Additional Supplies

Four 8" lace doilies, cut in half
Basting glue

Quilt Assembly

1. As they are needed, cut patches A–F, as listed in the Fabric Requirements table. (See the Rotary Cutting table for patch measurements.)

2. Referring to the block assembly diagram, make eight Chocolate Kisses blocks (fig. 1).

3. For the Lace Basket block, cut patches G–J. Cut the angles in the H, Hr, and I patches as described in the Hints section, on page 82. Sew G–I together to make a basket unit (fig. 2).

4. Align the raw edge of a half-doily with the long side of a J patch. Use dabs of basting glue to hold the doily in place. With monofilament or matching thread, machine appliqué the doily to the J patch. Then join the J patch to the basket unit. Make eight Lace Basket blocks (fig. 3).

5. Arrange the blocks as shown in the quilt assembly diagram, being careful to rotate them to achieve the desired design (fig. 4, page 82). Sew the blocks together in horizontal rows. Then sew the rows together.

6. For each side of the quilt, sew the inner and outer border strips together. Treat each combined strip as a single-border unit. Sew the border units to the quilt and miter the corners, being careful to match the seams at the miters.

7. Add batting and backing and baste the layers together. Quilt as desired.

This quilt is heavily quilted in the background areas with a closely spaced stipple in matching thread. Gentle arcs are sewn on top of the lace doilies to add dimension, and the basket bottoms and chocolate kiss X's are echo-quilted inside the triangle units with matching thread. The outer border has a continuous decorative design in pink thread.

8. Use your favorite method to bind the raw edges of the quilt with the 2¼" binding strips.

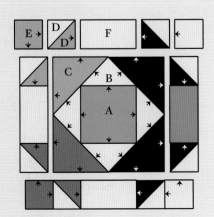

FIG. 1. Chocolate Kisses block

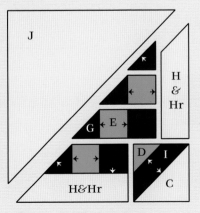

FIG. 2. Basket unit

FIG. 3. Lace Basket block assembly

Fig. 4. Quilt assembly

TRY THIS ...

You can purchase lace doilies at craft and sewing stores or even large discount chain stores. Or, you can use pretty antique hankies or salvage the undamaged sections of worn lace curtains or stained table scarves. Consider using fusible web to fill your baskets with fabric flowers or lace motifs, or you can machine or hand embroider your choice of lovely designs. Be creative. As another unique option, use broderie perse appliqués of delectable chocolate motifs to fill your baskets. The possibilities are endless.

Hints

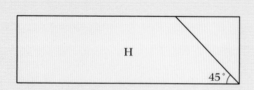

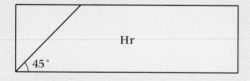

QUICK H/HR PATCHES

To make the H and Hr patches, use the 45-degree angle on your ruler to cut off the appropriate end of each 2" x 6⅞" rectangle.

QUICK I PATCHES

To make the I patches, cut both ends of each 1½" x 5½" rectangle at a 45-degree angle.

ADHESIVE CAUTION

I don't recommend using a basting spray or fusible web adhesive if the doily is lacy, because the sticky residue will be exposed, and it will adhere to the sole plate of your iron as you press. The residue will also attract lint and dust, which will make the doily look dirty.

Windows to Belgium

Known as the Venice of the North, Brugge is a picturesque city with a series of serene canals running through the town. The French pronunciation of Brugge rhymes with that popular Olympic bobsled-like sport, luge, but the Flemish pronunciation of the word is something I couldn't possibly begin to write phonetically! Boats and bicycles are the favorite forms of local transportation. An ancient stone wall surrounds and guards the perimeter of the city, and a splendid gate adorns the entrance. Shops selling the highest quality lace and tapestries line the pristine streets and canals, and the architecture of the buildings is simply magnificent.

Made with simple Attic Windows blocks, this little quilt provides the perfect way to showcase special memories from your vacation. This project is fast and fun and makes a great keepsake. For my souvenir quilt, I've chosen delicate lace appliqués from Brugge and the country's capital, Brussels. It's a wonderful remembrance of Belgium, one of the loveliest countries in Europe.

QUILT SIZE: 35" x 35"
FINISHED BLOCK SIZES: 6" x 6"

Windows to Belgium

WINDOWS TO BELGIUM, sewn and machine quilted by the author. The lace appliqués were purchased in Belgium.

84

Quilt A TRAVEL SOUVENIR *Kimberly Einmo*

Fabric Requirements

FABRIC	YARDS	PATCHES
Navy print (background)	½	16 A
Yellow 1	⅜	16 B
Medium blue 1	⅜	16 Br
Green	¾	18" square for bias-cut vine
		8 each of patterns 3 and 4
		16 each of patterns 7 and 8
Medium blue 2	¼	8 of pattern 2
		12 of pattern 6
Dark blue	⅛	12 of pattern 5
Yellow 2	¼	8 of pattern 1
		12 each of patterns 9 and 10
		4 each of patterns 11 and 12
White (inner border background)	½	4 strips 3½" x 32½"
Floral (outer border)	½	4 strips 3" x 37½"
Backing	1¼	39" x 39"
Binding	⅜	4 strips 2¼" x 42"
Batting		39" x 39"

ROTARY CUTTING
MEASUREMENTS INCLUDE SEAM ALLOWANCE

PATCH	MEASUREMENT
A	4¾" x 4¾"
B/Br	2¼" x 6⅞" (see Hints, Quick B/Br patches, page 87)

Additional Supplies

Light- or medium-weight fusible web
Lace appliqués, appliqué motifs, or
designs of your choice for the "windows"
Basting glue
⅜" bias bar for making the vine

Quilt Assembly

1. As needed, cut the patches listed in the Fabric Requirements table. (See the Rotary Cutting table for patch measurements.)

2. Referring to the block assembly diagram, make sixteen Attic Windows blocks (fig. 1).

3. Using monofilament or matching thread, machine appliqué the lace or embroidered motifs to the Attic Windows block centers.

4. Arrange the blocks as shown then follow the quilt assembly diagram to sew the blocks into horizontal rows. Join the rows (fig. 2).

5. For each side of the quilt, sew the inner and outer border strips together. Treat the combined strips as a single border unit. Sew the border units to the quilt and miter the corners, being careful to match the seams at the miters.

6. Cut ⅞"-wide bias strips from the 18" green square. Use the strips and the bias bar to make a continuous vine ⅜" wide.

7. Lightly trace the vine pattern on the border. Using a hot, dry iron, follow the tracing to fuse the continuous bias vine to the borders. Then fuse the appliqué pieces to the border.

8. With matching thread and a narrow zigzag stitch, finish the edges of the appliqués by hand or machine.

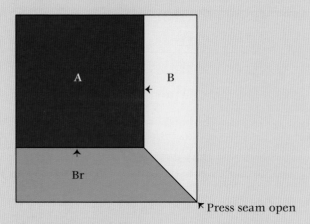

FIG. 1. Block assembly

FIG. 2. Quilt assembly

9. Add batting and backing then baste the layers together. Quilt as desired.

Windows to Belgium is lightly quilted in invisible thread over the entire surface. The window "panes" are free-motion quilted with continuous leaves and vines, and the borders are stitched in the ditch. The outer border is quilted with a loose, gentle stipple design.

10. Use your favorite method to finish the raw edges of the quilt with the 2¼" binding strips.

Hints

QUICK B/BR PATCHES

To make the B and Br (B reversed) patches quickly, and without having to use a template, cut the B/Br rectangles and place two of them wrong sides together. Use the 45-degree angle on your ruler to cut off one end, through both layers. This cut will produce one B and one Br piece.

ATTIC WINDOWS CORNER SEAM

1. The set-in seam at the corner of the Attic Windows block is really very simple. Be sure to mark a dot ¼" from the corner of your A patch, and ¼" from the end of both the B and Br patches, as shown in the figure.

2. Match the dots for sewing. Sew the B and Br pieces to the A square, ending the seams at the dot and leaving the seam allowances unsewn.

3. Fold the block in half on the diagonal, wrong sides together, to match the edges of the remaining seam. Sew from the dot outward to the corner. (See diagram on page 88.)

QUICK B/BR PATCHES

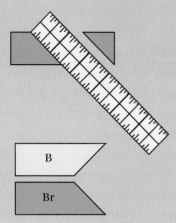

ATTIC WINDOWS CORNER SEAM

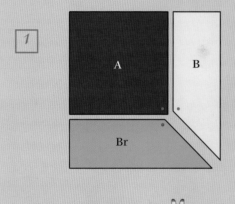

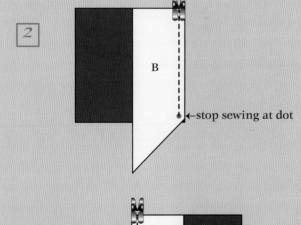

←stop sewing at dot

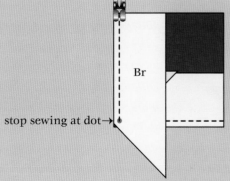

stop sewing at dot→

3

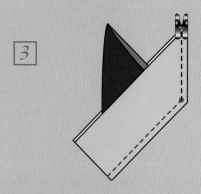

4.Press the diagonal seam allowances open to make the block lie flatter.

BAVARIAN HOLIDAY, sewn and machine quilted by the author

TRY THIS ...

If you own an embroidery machine, there are thousands of lace designs available on the market today that you could stitch onto your Attic Windows blocks. Or, you could hand embroider or cross-stitch designs of flowers, buildings, or landmarks in the block centers. Why not transfer special travel photos to fabric to be "seen" through the Windows (see photo at left)? Be creative and showcase your travel souvenirs. Add lace, buttons, an antique handkerchief, or small broaches and jewelry. The design possibilities are endless with this easy, yet classic quilt block.

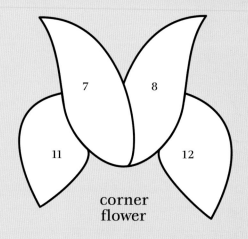

corner flower

flower 2

5

7 6 8

You do not need turn-
under allowances for fusible
web appliqué. If you prefer
turned edges, add a 3/16" allowance to fabric pieces.

9

4 3

2

1

flower 1

flower 2

10

9

10

10

9

10

flower 2

9

10

flower 1

QUILT SIZE: 52" x 52"

FINISHED BLOCK SIZES: 8" x 8" and 5" x 5"

FRUITS OF TUSCANY

FRUITS OF TUSCANY, sewn and machine embroidered by the author,
machine quilted by Carolyn Archer, Lebanon, Ohio.
The fruits were drawn by the author's father, Wilbur W. Wallace.

Italy seems to bask in golden sunshine every day of the year. Days are long and sun drenched, nights are damp and cool, and everything moves at an unhurried pace. The locals are gracious and warm, and the stresses of modern life seem non-existent. A sightseeing excursion through the remains of cities and buildings that date back centuries ago reminds visitors of once-great civilizations. Narrow cobbled streets, stone archways, and exquisite mosaic tiles linger among the rubble from ages past and lend a bit of mystique to an area rich in legend and tradition. Could those be ancient spirits or just the wind rustling through the olive trees?

The wonderful fabric used in the setting triangles and outer border inspired this quilt and captures the allure, essence, and romance of the Tuscan region exquisitely. The middle border is pieced with mosaic-style blocks, which echo the elegance of an Italian tile design. Vivid green symbolizes the lush landscape, rich blue reflects the cool azure of the Mediterranean Sea, and warm yellow captures the glorious sunshine. Outline embroidery, stitched in green, epitomizes the bounty of summer, when ripening fruits are fresh and plentiful.

FABRIC	YARDS	PATCHES
Yellow (background)	2	4 A, 8 B, 8 D, 4 E, 112 G, 4 I, 4 K, 9 N
Medium blue	⅛	8 A
Medium green	⅛	24 C
Gold	⅛	8 A
Dark green	½	32 F, 14 H, 2 J
Dark blue	½	24 F, 18 H, 2 J
Brown (borders 1 and 3)	⅜	8 strips 1" (see step 6 before cutting)
Multi-print (includes setting triangles and outer border)	1⅝	8 L, 4 M 2 strips 3½" x 46½" (cut parallel to selvages) 2 strips 3½" x 52½" (cut parallel to selvages)
Backing	3⅜	2 panels 29" x 56"
Binding	½	6 strips 2¼" x 42"
Batting		56" x 56"

ROTARY CUTTING
MEASUREMENTS INCLUDE SEAM ALLOWANCE

PATCH	MEASUREMENT
A	2½" x 2½"
B	5¼" x 5¼" (cut in quarters diagonally)
C	2⅞" x 2⅞" (cut in half diagonally)
D	2½" x 4½"
E	4⅞" x 4⅞" (cut in half diagonally)
F	1⅝" x 3½" (see Hints: Quick F and H patches, page 94)
G	use patterns on page 96
H	1⅝" x 7½" (see Hints: Quick F and H patches, page 94)
I, J, and K	use patterns on page 96
L	12¾" x 12¾" (cut in quarters diagonally)
M	6¾" x 6¾" (cut in half diagonally)
N	10" x 10" (trim to 8½" x 8½" after embroidering)
Embroidery	use patterns on pages 97–99

ADDITIONAL SUPPLIES

Embroidery floss
Or 12 wt. cotton thread

Quilt Assembly

1. As they are needed, cut the patches listed in the Fabric Requirements table. (See the Rotary Cutting table for patch measurements.)

2. Trace the fruit designs (pages 97–99) on the N squares. (Be sure to position the designs on point in the blocks.) Then embroider the designs by hand or machine. Trim the embroidered blocks to 8½".

3. Referring to the block assembly diagram, make four Italian Basket blocks (fig. 1). The sewn blocks need to be 8½" square including seam allowances.

4. For the lattice border, make twelve Old Italian blocks of version 1 and sixteen of version 2. Make two Old Italian corner blocks of version 1 and two of version 2 (fig. 2). The sewn blocks need to measure 5½" with seam allowances.

5. Arrange all the blocks and setting triangles as shown in the quilt assembly diagram (fig. 3, page 94). Sew them in diagonal rows then join the rows. Because the setting triangles are cut slightly large, trim the edges of the quilt, leaving ¼" seam allowances at all the points.

6. For the lattice border to fit, the quilt center needs to measure 34½" in both directions. If it doesn't, change the width of the brown "spacer" strips so that the quilt, including its first strip, will measure 35½".

7. Cut the eight brown border strips and join them, end to end, with diagonal seams. Measure your quilt and cut the strip into border lengths as needed. Sew the side inner border strips to the quilt then add the top and bottom strips.

8. For each side of the quilt, join seven Old Italian blocks, three of version 1 and four of version 2, alternating them to create the lattice effect.

FIG. 1. Italian Basket block assembly

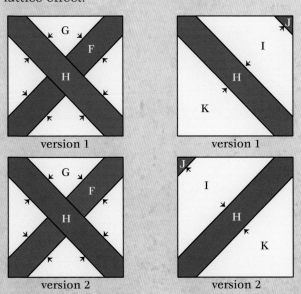

FIG. 2. Old Italian block, left, and Old Italian Corner block assembly

FIG. 3. Quilt assembly

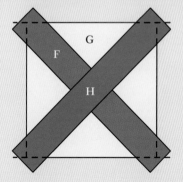

9. Sew the side lattice borders to the quilt first. Add the corner blocks to the ends of the remaining two lattice borders. (Be sure to rotate the corner blocks to complete the lattice.) Sew these borders to the top and bottom of the quilt. Press the seam allowances toward the border.

10. Sew the second brown spacer strip to the quilt as before. Then add the outer border.

11. Add the batting and backing and baste the layers together. Quilt as desired.

FRUITS OF TUSCANY is quilted with a 1½" crosshatch grid in the backgrounds of the fruit squares. The Italian Basket blocks are outline stitched with a decorative curved cross design in the four-patch centers, and the setting triangles feature a continuous decorative pattern. The Old Italian Blocks mimic the quilt center with outline quilting in the background triangles and a curved cross design in the centers. All the borders are stitched in the ditch.

12. Use your favorite method to bind the raw edges of the quilt with the 2¼" binding strips.

Hints

QUICK F AND H PATCHES

1. To make the F and H patches quickly and without having to use a template, cut the rectangles as listed in the Rotary Cutting table.

2. Use the rectangles to make the Old Italian blocks and corner blocks then trim the rectangles even with the edges of the blocks.

B/C UNITS

Sew the B/C units as shown and be sure to trim the "dog ear" points from the edges before sewing the units in the Italian Basket blocks. Trimming them will reduce bulk in the seams.

LET A SPECIAL FABRIC DO THE WORK

The mosaic print fabric used in the setting triangles and the outer border was the inspiration for this quilt. The outer border was carefully "fussy" cut from the fabric to make a single row of motifs. Look for a pretty border print or other wonderful feature fabric and let it do the work of complementing your mosaic-style blocks for extra pizzazz.

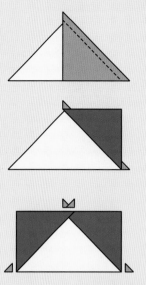

TRY THIS ...

Have you tried using your digitizing software program yet? The bold, clean lines of the fruit designs provide an easy place to begin. (Admit it – many of you own embroidery software and you haven't used the digitizing program because it seems intimidating.) This is the perfect opportunity to jump in and give it a try. Simply scan the fruit designs into the computer and follow the directions in your embroidery software owner's manual. Here are the basic steps to follow to digitize the designs:

1. Import the scanned image into your digitizing software.

2. Size your design.

3. Choose the thread color.

4. Select the auto trace / double trace option.

5. Save the design in the desired machine format.

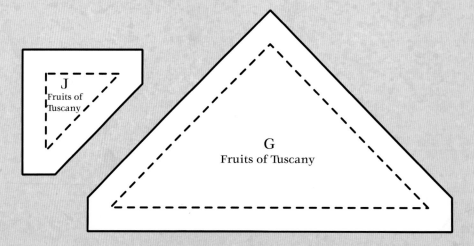

J
Fruits of
Tuscany

G
Fruits of Tuscany

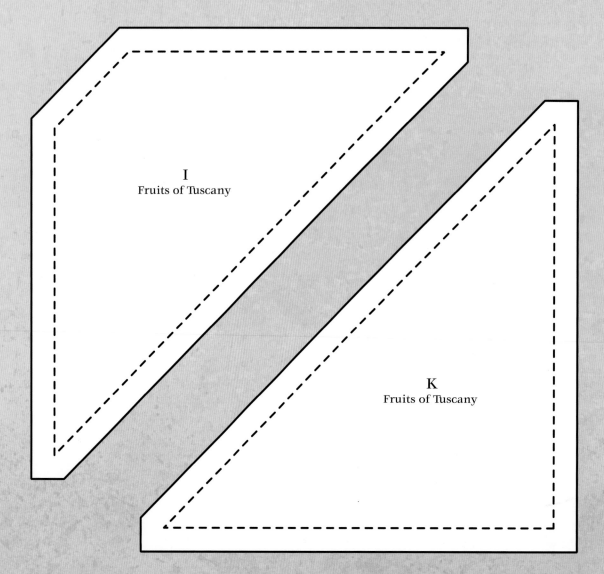

I
Fruits of Tuscany

K
Fruits of Tuscany

QUILT SIZE: 64" x 64"

FINISHED BLOCK SIZES: 8" x 8"

Greek Isle Cruise

GREEK ISLE CRUISE, sewn by Claire Neal, RAF Lakenheath, England,
and machine quilted by Carolyn Archer, Lebanon, Ohio.

An eastern Mediterranean cruise around the Greek Isles is like no other vacation you can imagine. The sea shimmers in so many breath-taking shades of blue that no words in the English language seem accurate enough to describe them. Each island beckons for you to come ashore to explore the many wonders and treasures just waiting to be discovered among the pristine white, domed buildings and quaint stone alleys. Taste-tempting trays of freshly baked baklava, dripping with honey, line bakery windows, and a wide variety of olives, meats, and cheeses are just waiting to be sampled and enjoyed while you relax beneath a shady tree. There is something about the mystique of the islands and the indescribable beauty of the ocean that seems to feed your soul. Cares simply float away on warm breezes.

This quilt is made with color-drenched batiks pieced in two simple, traditional blocks. The overall design is captivating in shades of aqua, blue, teal, and just a touch of olive green to add a shimmering sparkle, like sunshine on the Mediterranean Sea. The quilt may look complex, and only you will know how simple it is to piece together.

Fabric Requirements

Yardage is based on fabrics at least 42" wide. Cut all strips selvage to selvage.

FABRIC	YARDS	PATCHES
Light blue-green (background)	1¼	128 B, 32 C, 8 E
Dotted blue-green	⅜	64 B
Olive green	1¼	208 B, 8 F
Aqua	1⅛	88 B, 8 C, 24 D
Medium blue	1⅛	16 A, 8 E
Dark blue	1½	88 B, 32 C, 24 D, 4 E
Backing	4	2 panels 35" x 68"
Binding	⅝	7 strips 2¼" x 42"
Batting		68" x 68"

ROTARY CUTTING
MEASUREMENTS INCLUDE SEAM ALLOWANCE

PATCH	MEASUREMENT
A	4½" x 4½"
B	2⅞" x 2⅞" (cut in half diagonally)
C	2½" x 2½"
D	6⅞" x 6⅞" (cut in half diagonally)
E	17¼" x 17¼" (cut in quarters diagonally)
F	8⅞" x 8⅞" (cut in half diagonally)

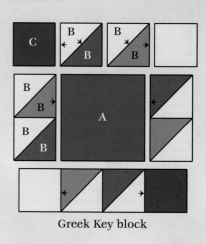

Greek Key block

FIG. 1. Block assembly

Quilt Assembly

1. As they are needed, cut the patches listed in the Fabric Requirements table. (See the Rotary Cutting table for patch measurements.)

2. Referring to the block assembly diagrams (fig. 1), make sixteen Greek Key blocks, sixteen Ocean Waves blocks (version 1), four Ocean Waves blocks (version 2), and four Ocean Waves blocks (version 3).

3. Assemble the blocks as shown in the quilt assembly diagram, being careful to rotate the blocks to achieve the desired interlocking design (Fig. 2, page 104). Sew the blocks together in horizontal rows. Then sew the rows together.

4. Carefully arrange E and F setting triangles as shown, and join them together to make four border units (fig. 3, page 104).

5. Sew the side border units to the quilt. Add Ocean Waves (version 1) blocks to each end of the remaining border units. Sew these units to the top and bottom of the quilt.

6. Add batting and backing and baste the layers together. Quilt as desired.

GREEK ISLE CRUISE was quilted on a longarm quilting machine. It features a custom-designed feather pattern in a beautiful, blue-teal variegated thread.

7. Use your favorite method to bind the raw edges of the quilt with the 2¼" binding strips.

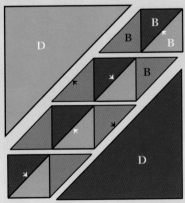
Ocean Waves block version 1

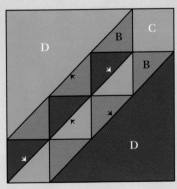
Ocean Waves block version 2

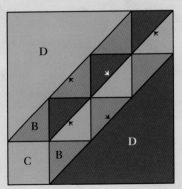
Ocean Waves block version 3

FIG. 1. Block assembly, continued.

FIG. 2. Quilt assembly

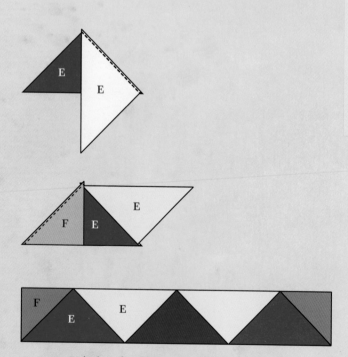

FIG. 3. Joining border triangles

Hint

CHECK UNIT SIZE

After sewing and pressing your pieces, such as the B half-square-triangle units, check to see that they measure exactly 2½" before joining them into blocks. Remake any that are significantly smaller and trim any that are larger than 2½".

TRY THIS ...

Thanks to speed piecing techniques, there are now more ways than ever to make half-square-triangle units fast and efficiently. You can try one of the special rulers or the triangle papers designed specifically for making these units. With these fast and efficient methods, you may find it easier to do away with cutting all those strips or using templates. Research and experiment with the different techniques to find the method you prefer.

Lesson Plans for Instructors

I hope many instructors will be inspired to teach classes featuring the quilts contained in this book. These quilts provide so many opportunities to teach various techniques and ways for students to improve their quiltmaking skills. The quilt designs can be easily adapted to highlight a regional historical event, local quilt retreat, or even a seasonal holiday. You might plan a quilt "scrapbooking" night at summer's end for students to gather together their own vacation souvenirs and showcase their memories in one of these quilts. And this is the perfect chance to encourage students to incorporate some of the fabulous features available on their mid- to high-end range of sewing and embroidery machines, especially if you are teaching at a sewing machine dealership. The creative possibilities are endless.

There are several options for teaching the classes, and I've included a few ideas to help you meet the needs of your students and the shop where you are teaching. It is a good idea to make a prerequisite that your students have at least some previous rotary-cutting and piecing experience before beginning a project from this book.

Please remember that the book's copyright prohibits photocopying or printing of any materials herein for commercial use. So please do not make photocopies of the patterns from this book to pass out to the students. Instead, have each student purchase her own copy of this book, or include the cost of the book in the class fee and make it part of the class supply list.

Class Overview

You might consider holding an orientation session, usually one or two hours, at least one week before the first hands-on sewing class. During the orientation, you can provide a class overview, then allow time for students to shop for fabric and supplies while you are available to assist them. This session can be optional rather than mandatory, because some students won't need any assistance. However, there are others who will truly appreciate your help in selecting the perfect fabrics for their individual projects. For some students, this is the most daunting task of making the quilt. It is much less stressful for them if the instructor is present with encouraging words and helpful advice to make them feel more at ease in making their color selections. As another benefit of holding an orientation session, you can review the supply list of items they will need to bring to class. It is frustrating for the teacher and other students when someone arrives for class who is not prepared or does not have the proper tools.

Three-Hour Classes

Ideal for holding on a weeknight (on consecutive weeks, if possible), this is a wonderful format for setting the pace and focusing on different techniques or skills during each session. You may want to hold two, three, four, or more weekly classes, depending on the size of the project and number of steps involved in completing the quilt. Simply adapt each weekly class to suit your own needs and teaching style. For example, if you will be using machine embroidery in the quilt or printing photos to fabric, you may want to focus on those techniques during an individual session and then focus on piecing the blocks, assembling the quilt top, quilting, etc., during subsequent classes.

RECOMMENDED QUILTS FOR TWO 3-HOUR CLASSES

PARISIAN PINWHEELS

Session 1. Piece the Pinwheel blocks and use a design wall to arrange color placement.

Session 2. Use class time to assemble the blocks into a quilt top, or have students assemble the quilt top at home before session 2 and work on machine quilting in class.

NOTTING HILL HIDDEN GARDEN

Session 1. Piece the Notting Hill blocks and begin the quilt top assembly.

Session 2. Use class time to machine quilt the top and practice machine embellishment techniques.

RECOMMENDED QUILTS FOR THREE 3-HOUR CLASSES

MARKET DAY

Session 1. Machine embroider the motifs on the blocks.

Session 2. Piece the Corn and Beans blocks.

Session 3. Use class time to assemble the quilt top, or have the students assemble the quilt top at home before session 3 then do machine quilting in class.

BOHEMIAN CRYSTAL

Session 1. Begin piecing the basic units needed for the blocks.

Session 2. Assemble the basic units to make Karlovy Vary and Variation blocks.

Session 3. Use class time to assemble the quilt top, or have the students assemble the quilt top at home before session 3 then do machine quilting in class. Discuss embellishment options.

ENGLISH ESTATE

Session 1. Begin piecing the basic units for the blocks.

Session 2. Assemble the basic units to make the Kings Crown, English Clover, and English Ivy blocks.

Session 3. Use class time to assemble the quilt top, or have students assemble the quilt top at home before session 3 then do machine quilting in class.

Recommended Quilts for four 3-Hour Classes

Ice Train to Amsterdam

Session 1. Piece the Windmill and Railroad blocks in class.

Session 2. Piece the Tulip blocks in class.

Session 3. Assemble the quilt top including the borders. Layer and baste the top, batting, and backing.

Session 4. Machine-quilt the layers. Focus on teaching different embellishment techniques and adding decorative stitches in class.

Keukenhof Tulips

Session 1. Piece the April Tulip blocks in class.

Session 2. Sew the Pieced Tulip blocks in class.

Session 3. Machine-appliqué the Tulip blocks in class and assemble the quilt top.

Session 4. Machine-quilt the layers in class and discuss embellishment options.

City of Lights

Session 1. Piece Paris Lights blocks, versions A and B, in class.

Session 2. Piece the Eiffel Steps and Twinkling Lights border blocks in class.

Session 3. Assemble the quilt top, including the pieced border. Layer and baste top, batting, and backing.

Session 4. Machine-quilt the layers in class and discuss decorative thread and embellishment options.

Memories of Germany

Session 1. Piece the Germany Star blocks and make bias strips for the pretzels and vines.

Session 2. Machine-embroider the corner blocks. Appliqué the pretzels and edelweiss.

Session 3. Machine-appliqué the grapes, leaves, and vines.

Session 4. Assemble the quilt top and discuss the quilting and embellishment options.

Chocolate and Lace

Session 1. Piece the Chocolate Kisses blocks.

Session 2. Machine-appliqué the lace and piece the Lace Basket blocks.

Session 3. Assemble the quilt top and add borders. Layer and baste the top, batting, and backing.

Session 4. Machine-quilt the layers in class and discuss embellishment options.

Fruits of Tuscany

Session 1. Machine-embroider the fruit motifs on the blocks. Discuss digitizing redwork-style embroidery with specialty software.

Session 2. Piece the Italian Basket and Old Italian blocks, versions A and B, in class.

Session 3. Assemble the quilt top, including the pieced and outer borders. Layer and baste top, batting, and backing together.

Session 4. Machine-quilt the layers in class and discuss embellishment options.

ONE-DAY WORKSHOPS

These classes work especially well if you hold them on Saturday or Sunday, or even from 6 p.m. to midnight on a Friday night. I find it helps to offer a potluck supper. Everyone brings a snack or dish to share with the other students and a drink for themselves. As the instructor, you might want to provide paper products, such as paper plates, napkins, and plastic cutlery. This format has been extremely successful for me because students relax and enjoy good food, friendship, and fun while they are learning and sewing, in an environment free from the distractions of home. They actually get a lot of sewing done in six to eight hours, and they leave class feeling a real sense of accomplishment, having been able to complete, or nearly complete, a quilt.

Assign some preparation work to your students before they come to an all-day class. Have them prepare and cut their fabrics in advance. You can even ask the students to machine-piece all the basic units at home, such as the half-square triangles and four-patches. These units are simple to make, however they can be tedious and time consuming. If this step is completed at home, you will be able to concentrate on teaching some of the more intricate details of assembling the blocks, and the students can do the quilting and embellishing in class.

RECOMMENDED QUILTS FOR ONE-DAY WORKSHOPS

TRIP TO DUBLIN
GREEK ISLE CRUISE

one day

Acknowledgments

To the following special friends who so generously gave of their time and talents to make some of the quilts featured within the pages of this book:

...Judy Schrader, your talent as a quilter simply shines in TRIP TO DUBLIN. Thank you so much for sharing your math expertise in helping me write this book. You are such a true and genuine friend, and you have helped me to attain so many of my goals, both in quilting and in life. You opened your home and your heart to me, my family, and our cats, and I am forever grateful!

...Claire Neal, you are one of the sweetest, most considerate friends I know. I'm so thankful you shared your exquisite workmanship and excellent eye for color in making GREEK ISLE CRUISE and KEUKENHOF TULIPS for this book. You have such a gift for creating beautiful things.

...Mary Flynn, thank you so much for sharing your heart, your friendship, and your confidence with me. You made ENGLISH ESTATE not only once, but twice! I'm so grateful for all the terrific ideas, tips and shortcuts you have shared with me, and I am in awe of your incredible talent for all things quilting.

...Carla Conner, thank you for your boundless generosity, sweet smile, and for always making me laugh. I consider myself lucky to have you as my friend. You are very talented, as evidenced by your outstanding work on CHOCOLATE AND LACE. You have what it takes to be a fantastic designer.

I am extremely grateful to the following individuals for their influence and involvement:

...Wendy Martin, my dear and true friend. Thank you for all the laughter, support, encouragement, and lunch outings to help me keep my sanity while I was working on this book. I will treasure your friendship always.

...Carolyn Archer, Owner, Ohio Star Quilting, Inc., Lebanon, Ohio. Your exquisite machine quilting put the sparkle and zing in many of the featured quilts, and I'm so grateful for your time, talent, and creative vision. I'd also like to thank Carolyn's husband, Bruce Archer, for designing original quilting motifs especially for several of the quilts featured in this book.

...Madeline Shepperson, Owner, Quilt-N-Stuff, Alexandria, Virginia. Thank you for giving me my start in quilting, first as a student, then as an employee, and finally as an instructor at your wonderful shop.

...Barbara Zygiel, my first quilting instructor. You taught me the fundamentals of quiltmaking that have been the foundation for everything I do today. Thank you for igniting the creative spark that continues to burn brightly.

...Carol Miller, Roseanne Mamer, and Lynn Miller, a million thanks for stepping up to sew my patterns "just one more time" so I could be sure of their accuracy. Each of you came through for me in so many ways, and I am blessed by the gift of your friendship and creativity.

...Pfaff Sewing Machines, VSM Sewing, Inc., Westlake, Ohio. I'm incredibly grateful for the opportunity to represent you as one of your Pfaff Sewing Stars. Thank you for the support of your many talented educators and for the use of your top-of-the-line machine, the Creative 2144 and 3-D software suite.

...Barbara Smith, my wonderful editor at AQS, and the entire AQS Creative Team. Thank you from the bottom of my heart for believing in the potential of my designs and for helping me to interpret so beautifully the vision in my mind's eye for this book.

I'd also like to thank all the wonderful students who have taken my classes over the years. I'm so grateful to have had the opportunity to witness your creativity and share the laughter and fun. I can honestly say I've learned something new from you with every class I have ever taught!

And last but certainly not least, I'm especially grateful for the following family members:

...William Lee Wallace, my brother. My heartfelt thanks for being so supportive as I embarked on this journey and for your endless hours of proofreading the manuscript.

...Wilbur and Nina Wallace, my parents. Thank you for introducing me to the joys of traveling. You have always believed in me and encouraged me to expand my horizons and to reach for the stars. I love you both.

...Joshua and Andrew Einmo, my wonderful sons. I appreciate your support and patience with me as I worked to meet deadlines and for enduring less-than-perfect meals so I could sew "just a little while longer." You are both so precious to me and are the best reminder where my priorities really lie.

...Kent Alan Einmo, my loving husband and best friend. You are my hero. I could never have come this far without your love and unwavering support. Thank you for taking me to destinations I only dreamed about before I married you. I'd go around the world and back again just to be by your side. I love you now and forever!

Resources

PFAFF SEWING MACHINES / VSM SEWING, INC.
31000 Viking Parkway
Westlake, OH 44145
www.pfaff.com
Pfaff sewing and embroidery machines, sergers, and embroidery software

DEN HAAG AND WAGENMAKERS
N.Z. Voorburgwal 97-99
1012 RE Amsterdam,
the Netherlands
www.dutchquilts.com
Authentic Dutch reproduction fabrics, toiles and Provencal print reproductions

LE ROUVRAY
3 Rue de la Bucherie
F-75005 Paris, France
www.lerouvray.com
French fabrics from Provence and toiles

FROM MARTI MICHELL PRODUCTS / MICHELL MARKETING, INC.
P.O. Box 80218
Atlanta, GA 30366-0218
770-458-6500
www.frommarti.com
A wide selection of Perfect Patchwork System Templates, rulers, books and other specialty tools

THE ELECTRIC QUILT COMPANY
419 Gould Street, Suite 2
Bowling Green, OH 43402-3047
800-356-4219
www.electricquilt.com
Electric Quilt 5, Blockbase, Stash and other quilting computer software

SULKY OF AMERICA INC.
3113 Broadpoint Drive
Harbor Heights, FL 33983
www.sulky.com
A wide variety of sewing and embroidery threads, stabilizers, books and notions

YLI CORPORATION
161 West Main Street
Rock Hill, SC 29730
www.ylicorp.com
Specialty threads for sewing and embroidery and a variety of silk ribbons

ROBISON-ANTON TEXTILE CO.
175 Bergen Boulevard
Fairview, NJ 07022
www.robison-anton.com
A large selection of sewing and embroidery threads in a wide range of colors and different size spools

KANDI CORP.
2036 Weaver Park Drive
Clearwater, FL 33765
800-985-2634
www.KandiCorp.com
The Lorna hot-fix applicator, studs, crystals, fusibles and other embellishment products

AMERICAN & EFIRD, INC.
24 American Street / P.O. Box 507
Mt. Holly, NC 28120
http://www.amefird.com
Manufacturers of Mettler and other name brand threads, yarns and notions

EZ QUILTING BY WRIGHTS
P.O. Box 398
West Warren, MA 01092-0398
www.ezquilt.com
A wide variety of acrylic rulers and rotary cutting accessories

OHIO STAR QUILTING, INC.
2895 Wilmington Rd.
Lebanon, OH 45036
(513) 933-9008
Ohiostarquilting@hotmail.com
Beautiful longarm machine quilting by Carolyn Archer

SEW-A-LOT
232 N Main St.
Centerville, OH
(937) 433-7474

QUILT-N-STUFF
5962 Richmond Hwy.
Alexandria, VA
(703) 960-8344

About the Author

Kimberly learned to sew at the age of seven and sewed many of her own clothes through her college years at Miami University in Oxford, Ohio. In 1991, she took the first of many quilting classes at Quilt-N-Stuff in Alexandria, Virginia, and then began working part-time at the shop, along with managing a full-time career as a graphic designer and publisher for an international trade association. In 1996, she began teaching classes and started creating her own original quilt designs. She developed a highly popular series of Mystery Quilt classes, which she has taught nationally and internationally.

Although she devotes a great deal of time designing quilts and teaching quilting and machine embroidery classes, her other favorite "hobby" is traveling. She has been to many of the fifty states and has traveled throughout the world, visiting more than twenty-five foreign countries in Europe, Asia, and Africa. From 2000 to 2004, she and her family lived in Germany where they spent a lot of time traveling extensively within the European community.

She loves to design quilts related to her travels. She represents VSM Inc. as a Pfaff Sewing Star, and her quilts and articles have appeared in various publications. Her goal is to travel all over the world teaching at guilds, quilt shows, and on quilting cruises to many destinations, including Bermuda, Hawaii, Alaska, and Australia. When not traveling, Kimberly resides with her husband, Kent, their two sons, two cats, and a dog in Kettering, Ohio.

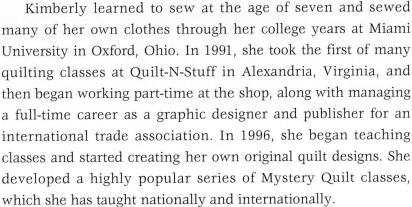

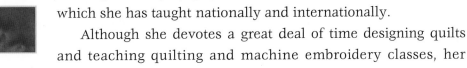

Other AQS Books

This is only a small selection of the books available from the American Quilter's Society. AQS books are known worldwide for timely topics, clear writing, beautiful color photos, and accurate illustrations and patterns. The following books are available from your local bookseller, quilt shop, or public library.

#6904   us$21.95

#6897   us$22.95

#6903   us$19.95

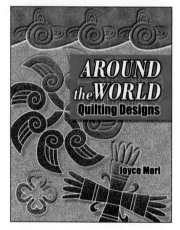

#6806   us$21.95

#6902   us$22.95

#6514   us$21.95

#6799   us$22.95

#6802   us$21.95

#6510   us$21.95

Look for these books nationally.
Call or **Visit** our Web site at

1-800-626-5420
www.AmericanQuilter.com